I0486981

# Desiree's

# Dreams

Desiree

Davidson

Desire Davidson

# CONTENTS

*Desire Davidson*

# New Friends

The girl who answered the door was a living doll. She had long brown hair swept back by a green hair band. Her eyes were a light grey. Her face was beautiful and what a figure, revealed in a white eyelet blouse tied at midriff and a pair of emerald green short shorts revealing great legs and the soft contours of an inviting cunt. She was braless and her large hard nipples were jutting out through the fabric. She had an ivory complexion which was repeated in her arms and long legs. She was about 5 feet 5 inches and all of her was hot. In short, she was drop-dead gorgeous!

"Hello," I said, "I'm Eric."

"I'm Janet," she said as she invited me in.

"James will be back in about 20 minutes-he had to run to the store," she said.

"I hope you'll like the meal I've made tonight it's a simple homemade Chinese dinner,"

Janet said, "Come sit at the kitchen table."

"James said you're from Oklahoma."

"We're both from the same town in Tennessee," she said.

I sat down at the table and positioned myself so the bulge in my pants wasn't so obvious. I had gone rock hard the minute I saw her. I wondered how I could have this sweet little doll. As I was thinking of how I might seduce her, she was telling me about the town where they both grew up and said they were high school sweet hearts. James was 22 and she was 21.

I loved to look at her and she loved to show off her beautiful body. She came over to the table and leaning over to set the places the three unbuttoned buttons of her blouse gave me a beautiful view of her 34-C breasts; almost exposing her nipples, which I noted were hard.

I was thinking about how nice it would be to fondle and kiss and suck her lovely breasts and nipples. Just then I heard the apartment door and James came in with a jar of Chinese mustard.

"Hi Eric, I'm glad you could make it through the snow. At least it's Friday and we won't have to get out tomorrow to go to Weapons Systems Control School", he said.

I noticed his words implied I would be spending the night.

"I'd love to spend the night with his wife and him, and do a lot more than sleep!" I thought.

Soon Janet had everything ready and we sat down to a delicious meal. As we ate they asked me to tell them of my life in Oklahoma and how I ended up in the Navy. They then reciprocated and told me about their life in Tennessee.

Toward the end of the meal, I said, "James, you didn't tell me you had a great cook and a drop-dead gorgeous wife!"

Janet said, "I'm glad you liked it and me."

That made me do a double take for I suspected I was about to experience a reverse pickup.

James and Janet cleaned up the table and kitchen, and I watched as they moved back and forth. They were well matched. James was about six feet and had a head of curly black hair. He was toned but not overly muscled. The outline of his body in his clothes showed a well proportioned man with weight to height just right. Anyone would call him extremely handsome and well matched with his sexy bride.

Things were completed in the kitchen and James said, "Let's go in the living room."

James and Janet sat down on the couch, so James and I were seated on either side of her. We talked some more and got to know each other. I was at one point absent mindedly thinking how much I'd like to fuck Janet when my hand brushed her left breast as I was talking with my hands.

I said "Oh, I'm sorry."

Janet replied, "Don't be sorry, I'm proud of them and looks like you liked the experience." As she said this, she reached over with one finger and lightly outlined my hard cock bulging down my right pant leg.

"I'm highly complimented," she said.

She took her finger away and I swear if my cock wasn't harder and longer than it had ever been.

James said, "Janet went to Chicago this week and bought a few things; she hasn't modeled them for me yet. Would you like to see a brief fashion show?"

Before I could reply, Janet said, "Yes Eric I want to do it for you. You can tell me if they are sexy enough."

Janet got up and went in the bedroom.

I wondered what could be sexier than the outfit she was wearing at dinner! I was about to find out: She came out in a red bikini which was just great with her brown hair. The top was not padded and her beautiful breast filled the cups perfectly and her large erect nipples were plainly outlined through the unlined top. Janet turned for us and struck several provocative model type poses.

Then she went back to the bedroom and shortly returned in a sheer light green baby doll pajama. She was wearing next to nothing and I could practically see all of her beautiful charms. She went through the same modeling routine and then came back a third time.

This time, Janet was wearing a cream colored cross between a baby doll bottom in its sheerness and a bikini bottom. There were little green ribbons at each side to release the panty. The top was even better. It was a little jacket with three green ribbons arrayed down the front. She looked fantastic as she modeled the outfit for us. I noticed as she showed the last outfit to us she released the top two ribbons. James and I both told her we liked the outfit she had on, best of the three. Janet instead of returning to the bedroom came back to the couch and sat down between us.

As she sat down she said, "I want to really see what effect I have on you two sailors."

I was hard and wanted her and I think the couple intended for me to have her, but I wasn't sure how to proceed. I decided to let them take the lead.

We returned to talking about everything of the life of a sailor and his wife. I could hardly keep my eyes off Janet's breasts.

Suddenly, James reached over and un-tied the last ribbon and pulled the sides away so her firm breasts were totally exposed. Then he said, "If you want them, take them. In fact you can fuck her if you want."

"Did I ever!" I thought.

I asked Janet if I could kiss her while I fondled her breasts and was answered by her pulling me toward her for a deep French kiss. The whole time I was fondling her breasts and kissing her, her small hand was stroking my cock through my pants. I moved down and began to suck her nipples as she continued to stroke my cock.

After about five minutes, Janet said, "Let's get you sailors out of your clothes so I can return the favor.

When I stood up, James was already naked and presenting a 7-inch average thickness dick.

Janet took the filmy little top off and tossed it to her husband but still had on the filmy bottom with the little green ribbons on each side. I finished removing all but my shorts. When I removed them and stood up my hard cock stood proudly against my belly and was seeping
pre-cum.

"Janet said, Oh god! James, look at the size of his cock. You two set on the couch for a minute, I want to suck you both--that is if I can get my mouth around the girl's delight he's packing."

James and I sat down on the couch and Janet kneeled in front of us. As she was getting down, James reached over and took my cock in his hand and stroked it and gauged its thickness.

"Janet is going to love this--so would I," James said.

Janet had not eaten any dessert at dinner and she joked, "Now, It looks like I get double helpings of whipped cream."

Janet started on her husband and in a short time made him come. She kept his cum in her mouth and came to me and kissed me so we could share his cum.

When she pulled away from my mouth she said, "My husband usually comes pretty fast. I can suck and fuck all night with a man equipped like you."

As she said it, she was cupping my big balls and commenting, "I bet these guys can keep on going. You are very well equipped!"

Janet began to suck me and was struggling to take me in, so I suggested we play another game. I stood up and then helped her to her feet. I said I was ready to fuck her now.

James got up and walked over with his dick limp and although his dick was slightly above average length erect, his balls were much smaller than average. I had noted in my mind the quantity of cum was small as she shared his cum with me in our deep kiss.

He stood behind Janet and pulled the ribbons and took the bottom garment away. He said, "Eric you can have my wife. I'd like to watch, if it's OK with you. Do anything you want with her short of anal or pain."

I picked Janet up and carried her to the bed. I was not surprised it was turned down for this moment. James followed us in and sat down on a chair. I lay Janet down on the bed and moved between her legs to fuck her face to face. She reached for my cock to position it in her wet pussy. I told her to stop and I asked her husband to take my cock and position it--thus he officially gave me his wife!

She was very wet and ready. I entered her gently. I moved with very gentle motion allowing her to adjust to my cock. When I was fully in, I paused and leaned down and kissed her and asked if she was ready for a good long fuck.

"I'm always ready to fuck as many men as I can get" she said.

"That was an interesting comment," I thought.

Maybe this pretty baby was a nymphomaniac, or hopefully just a normal woman who could never get enough sex. I began to fuck her and I could feel she had a large clit which was being rubbed with my every thrust. About five minuets after I started fucking her, she had her first vaginal orgasm and then just kept on coming for the next fifteen minutes, when I began to shoot long jets of cum into her pretty little body. She felt so good and her beautiful routine of setting this up had me super excited and I shot about seven streams into her cunt. I knew what James wanted from his behavior. I told him to come to his wife and lick the cum out of her cunt. While he was doing that, I told him when he was through, he was to clean my cock of his wife's delicious juices and then suck my cock back up to maximum firmness so I could fuck Janet again.

As James sucked my cock hard again, his techniques made it obvious that mine wasn't the first cock he had sucked. He was definitely bisexual. While he sucked my cock, Janet and I were deep kissing and I was playing with her beautiful breasts. She was a great kisser and I suspected very oral when the cock wasn't quite so large. I held her away from me and I asked if she would like me to cum in her husband's mouth.

She said, "He'll love it, I've seen him take several guys in turn at a party, but what I'd really like, is to watch you fuck his virgin ass!"

James continued to suck and in my mind I speeded up my excitement and began to shoot stream after stream of cum into his mouth. He was in heaven having gotten two loads of cum, one from his wife's pussy and one directly from me while sucking off the man who had fucked her.

We took a break and mostly Janet and I talked as we drank our cokes. It seemed James and Janet held sex parties very frequently with usually 10 to 12 men who had been selected by James from the naval base personnel or occasionally one or two Marines from the group that was stationed at the Ninth Naval District for security and entrance guard detail. They had been doing it for almost a year.

James went to the bathroom and we were alone. Janet told me her husband wanted to try anal sex. He took her that way and she thoroughly enjoyed it. I asked if she would like to have me anally fuck both of them. She said yes, but James had never allowed another man to take her ass, although he did it regularly. She told me the reason he still had a virgin ass was he had not yet felt comfortable enough with any one of my men. I think he is comfortable with you.

I told her I would love to be the first man to take her husband and I wanted her to participate when the time came. She told me she would. James returned in a few minutes and it was a few minutes more before we retuned to the bedroom.

Janet told her husband to suck my semi-hard cock to get it fully hard and ready. He went at the task with a passion.

While he was sucking me off, Janet said, "Eric would like to be the first to take your virgin ass. She went on and told him if he was satisfied with the experience she would like to give her ass to me as well"

James said, "I would like to try you and you can have my wife anytime, but no one else but you and me."

When he had me fully hard, I told James to lie on his side so I could lubricate his anus with the Vaseline Janet brought to me. I stretched him with lubricated fingers until three fingers entered easily. He was relaxed and ready.

I had Janet lubricate the head of my cock
and the entire shaft. Her talented hands
stroked my cock and it felt wonderful.
When lubrication was completed, I asked
James to lie on his back with his legs
open. As he took the position, I noted
his dick was only semi-hard. I lifted his
legs over my shoulders and asked Janet to
take my cock and guide me as I entered
him, and in this way symbolically give me
her husband to fuck.

She held my cock and I gently entered
head deep. Then I allowed him to relax,
and I eased past his sphincter muscle and
gently pushed in the full length of my
cock. I asked if he was ready. He said
yes and I told Janet to lay her head on
his stomach and take his dick in her
mouth and suck him off while I fucked
him. I began to take long slow strokes
and just as he cried out he was coming. I
went to rapid thrusts and raised my
excitement level so my cock began to
shoot cum into his ass. James was no
longer a virgin. He was a confirmed
bisexual. I pulled out of him and went to
the bathroom to cleanup. When I returned,
James headed for the bathroom.

While James went to the bathroom,
Janet and I made out kissing and
fondling. I asked her if she was ready to
have another man's cock in her ass. I
would love it, but let's ask James if he
is sure, again. When James returned I
asked him if he would give me his
beautiful wife's ass. He eagerly said he
wanted me to be her second in and asked
if he could be involved. I told him he
would do the same thing to give his wife
to me as she had done, and after he had

guided me in, he could fondle her breasts and kiss her while I fucked her.

I pulled Janet's beautiful legs over my shoulders and James took my cock and guided it as I entered her. Janet had never been stretched this much so I went very slowly. When she was relaxed I began long swift thrusts and rocked her world. She started coming just like she did when I was in her cunt--she was truly a hot little number--orgasmic in every department. She was wonderful. She literally milked cum out of my body with her anal muscles. What a sexy doll!

When I finished, I went to the bathroom to clean up. When I came back it was almost as if they didn't expect me to come back so soon, for they were talking in hushed tones.

They looked up and Janet said, "Would you spend the night with us and stay with us through Saturday too?"

I told them yes, I would love to be with them. Where will I sleep?" I asked.

Janet said, "You will sleep with me and if you want my husband you can take him in the living room on the thick, soft rug."

James said, "We want you to take us separately or together in any way you choose."

Janet went to the bathroom to clean up and gave me the chance to make fully sure James was alright with what Janet said and he was in full agreement.

When Janet came back, I proposed we have one more together session before I took her to a single man bed.

I said, "I want James and me to do a double penetration of your pussy."

Janet was concerned about my cock size but was ready to try. I had James lay on the bed on his back. I sucked his dick a few minutes to get him totally hard and then I had Janet impale herself on him with her face looking at his feet. I then eased her back so she was totally lying with her back on her husband's chest. James's dick was firmly in her about four inches. I had them spread their legs and I kneeled over the couple and placed my cock against James's dick and slowly opened up Janet's cunt. I felt the head of my cock move over the head of James's dick and I thrust in several more inches. I had James make short rapid thrusts in his wife while I took longer thrusts.

My cock was pressed against her clit with every thrust and very soon the pretty baby was coming on us. In only a short time, James began to shoot his cum. I felt the warmness of his cum coat my cock. His dick softened fairly rapidly and he pulled out leaving his wife for me to finish as he held her. I fucked the beautiful bitch for several more minutes and then proceed to fill her cunt with cum.

We separated and the three of us lay on our sides together. James was behind Janet and Janet and I were facing.

I asked, "Are you sure you want to have sex in separate rooms?"

They both agreed it was what they wanted. I asked James to move off the bed. Then I placed Janet on her back. My cock was hard again and I had James once again give me his wife by placing and guiding my cock into her pussy. As we fucked I heard the bedroom door open and close and we were truly alone. When I finished in her, I had her kneel over my face so I could lick my cum out of her cunt and stimulate her clit with my tongue to bring her to some mind blowing chain orgasms.

It was already early morning and I had been cuddling Janet in my arms for a couple of hours.

She got up to use the bathroom and when she returned she said she wanted to sleep for awhile. When she was asleep, I left the bedroom and went to the living room and found James awake and waiting.

I prepped him with lubricant and had James stand by the sofa and lean over the arm. I was already hard having cuddled Janet's sexy little body. I placed my cock against a well lubricated ass and shoved my cock into James. After a few minutes of thrusting his dick shot cum into the side of their sofa, as my large cock had massaged his prostate to orgasm. I fucked him for about 15 minutes and then I blasted off in him. He really felt good and if I closed my eyes I could imagine my cock's next turn at Janet.

James and I went to the bathroom and I made him clean me up. I left and he finished up himself. When he returned I had a ready cock for him to suck. He obviously had lots of practice for he was adept at orally pleasuring a man.

I went back to the bedroom and found Janet on her side. As I cuddled her my hardening cock was pressed into her legs just below her cunt. As she slept, I pulled her legs up to gain entry as we spooned. I fucked her gently for a long time. The gorgeous bitch had orgasms in her sleep and did not wake. As I was also growing sleepy, I stepped up the pace and filled her cunt with cum.

The next morning, my hosts were rejuvenated and ready for more sexual play and it continued well into Saturday night.

On Saturday afternoon, they got out their photo album and showed me photos of their parties which always lasted from 8 o'clock Friday evening until 2 o'clock Saturday afternoon about once a month. The photos confirmed Janet took between 10 and 12 men at each of their parties. I was an invited guest at their next party and quite the star!

*Desire Davidson*

# Educational Bondage

Kathryn was coming down the hall from her office. Jennifer, 'my first love,' had introduced us at a school activity sometime before, and I had placed her on my list to hunt. She was the Principal of the K-6 elementary school where Jennifer was a third grade teacher.

Kathryn was beautiful with long black hair and grey eyes complementing her beautiful tall, slender frame. Her face was regal and her attitude was of caring ownership of her school. She had been married when she was 18 and it didn't last--she had joked with Jennifer that it was because he couldn't last!

Kathryn came up to me and said, "Move along sailor we don't have anything but little grade school girls here--won't meet you needs."

I asked,"Where should I move along to?"

She said, "I suggest my office."

There were twenty minutes left before Jennifer would let her third grade students out, so I readily followed her.

Kathryn sat down behind her desk and I took a chair in front.

I said, "I didn't come here for a little grade school girl--I came for a teacher and perhaps a Principal too!"

"Be careful Eric," She said, "We still do corporal punishment here you know!"

She opened a desk drawer and pulled out a small paddle.

I said, "It's too little for a scoundrel like me."

She walked around the desk and said, "Let's see!"

I stood up and met her halfway. I bent over for her and she could see my wallet protected my left buttock, so she swung into my right. The smack gave me an instant erection!

Kathryn had me stand up. "God," she said, "You are hung!"

I asked, "Do I detect an interest there?"

She replied, I have an interest, but I have three parent conferences I need to get ready for. It is a shame she said, I would have let you take me right here on my desk.

She said, "You better go, the last bell of the day is about to ring."

A few weeks later it was a Saturday afternoon and Jennifer had gone to a church function. I walked her over on the crunchy snow where the sidewalks hadn't been cleared yet and I decided to walk the town square on the way back. Kathryn was coming out of a jewelry and accessories store.

I greeted her with, "Did you buy anything you'd like to model for me?"

"As a matter of fact, I did, but you'd need at least two hours to get the full effect," she said.

I told her I had two hours, because Jennifer was at a church function for the afternoon.

"Good," she said, "you can come home with me and I'll model my purchases."

She had some other things in her car and I carried them in when we arrived at her house. Her house was much like Jennifer's--an updated Victorian.

Kathryn invited me to set down in the living room. It was very pretty and it spoke of a much disciplined person, but there were little romantic features to the furnishings of the room.

Shortly she came down stairs in a soft v-neck, cream colored, satin blouse showing the tops of her ample breasts. She wore a skirt that struck about 6 inches above the knee, it was a pretty emerald green satin and was full. Her black hair was pulled back by a matching green satin ribbon and she was wearing a bright red lipstick on her full lips, and a beautiful necklace of gold and green and grey hung around her neck--the same shade of grey as her eyes. She was a doll!

I let out a whistle and said, "Wow, you're beautiful."

She came and sat down by me and we began to kiss--softly exploring, and then we went to passionate kisses. My free hand was exploring her legs and suddenly she said, I think its time to take this sailor upstairs for a little discipline.

Kathryn led me upstairs to her bedroom. Everything was romantic there. The bed had been turned back for my expected arrival. She had me sit in a lovely Victorian chair in the corner and told me I was being punished; I had to remain in the chair for a time-out. I took my seat and she told me she was going to take her clothes off for me. She took her skirt off and hung it up, then the blouse and she was standing before me in high heels, stockings, garter belt, panties and bra, all coordinated as bright red except the stockings were very sheer silver grey. She removed her heels, released her stockings and rolled them down her shapely legs, then released her bra. She was a D-Cup but surprisingly firm (I would soon find they were silicon enhanced). She had large nipples and areola and I was ready to have them as soon as they were shown. Kathryn then removed her garter belt and then the panties and she stood fully nude before me. My cock was straining to be free.

She walked toward me and said, "Now you have seen what I have to offer are you still interested?"

I stood up to kiss her and she pushed me back. She told me she would stand before me and I could play with anything she had to offer but I could not get out of the chair.

I was never so grateful for having long arms and long fingers. I touched her every where except her lips. After about 10 minutes she let me undress and my long thick cock was finally against her warm body.

Kathryn led me to her bed and I moved in beside her to continue kissing, but she told me she was ready for sex.

I moved between her legs and she took my cock and guided me into her pussy. It was marvelous--wet, ready, and deliciously tight. In a few minutes my beautiful Principal was coming on me. I kept right on fucking her and she kept right on coming. After about 20 minuets I could delay the inevitable no longer and I began to come with her. I filled her delightful little pussy with enough cum for three average men.

Kathryn was amazing. It was a fun afternoon.

*Desire Davidson*

After Jennifer died of a brain tumor
on the 22nd of January, 1972, I went to
Kathryn for comfort and it was there I
got control of my emotions and began to
see things objectively and with intense
passion. She started the healing process
for me. I spent numerous nights in her
bed through February and most of March
and was loved in spirit and passion as I
grieved for Jennifer.

*Desire Davidson*

# Naughty or Nice

At the beginning of our marriage, you suggested we include others in our love making but when I was negative about a 'play date' you backed away as if it wasn't that important to you.

I was teaching high school English and there was this man English teacher who challenged my academics and the morals I was attempting to incorporate in my lessons. For some reason he was very hot to me, maybe it was because he contended with me over everything. I told you about him, and you began to tease me that he was the one for my first experience. I resisted, but my resolve wavered; I found myself turned on all day and looking forward to talking to him after school, and yes flirting with him when he would stop by my classroom at the end of the day. School ended at 3 and you got home after 6:30 pm consistently and many times he and I would talk forever."

You teased me and encouraged me and one day I came home with a few things from the drug store, and there was a box of condoms. I had decided and they went in my purse, but they were never used.

Before I put them away, you held them up and said, "Just so you'll know, these are worthless, manufacturers don't make one big enough for Stan." You said, "You'll just have to take him bareback like you have me for the 4 years you've been off birth control pills. If he impregnates you, its no big deal--we'll

have the baby we've been wanting." I was
not the least put off by what you said,
and over the next week I became more
seductive in my flirting. I talked to you
about wanting to be alone at first and
then have you join in, and you supported
every thing I wanted and encouraged my
determination.

The following Saturday, we went to
Oklahoma City and bought new beautiful
sheer lingerie, garter belt and
stockings. The panties had ribbon ties at
the sides, so they could be removed
without removing anything else. The bra
had front closure. You bought a beautiful
silk cream blouse, low cut and button
down the front. A pretty pastel blue mini
skirt coordinated with the lingerie. The
pastel blue high, high heels which
matched a new hand bag, coordinated with
everything. When you put it on at home
with your pale pink choker pearls you
were a living doll!

Monday, there was nothing. Tuesday
there was nothing. Wednesday there was
nothing, and then Thursday came and I was
dressed for a seduction. Eric, I went to
school with the intent of seducing him.
As it turned out the seduction was more a
mutual agreement thing. School ended and
Stan came into my room, he closed the
door and locked it. The blinds were down
and we were alone. He walked over to my
chair. As he approached, he told me how
beautiful I looked in the new outfit. He
stood by my chair. I could see Stan's
huge erection outline and as he slid his
hand into my bra and cupped my breast, I
reached for his erection. He removed his
hand, lifted me up and kissed me

passionately several times. He told me he wanted me, and I confirmed I wanted him. What happened next surprised me. Luckily there was nothing breakable on my desk, for he swept everything off. He laid me down on the desk. I thought condom-then I realized he was even bigger than you Eric. I had been wet all day and I was ready! He slowly un-buttoned my blouse and opened my front close bra exposing my breasts, he lifted me and slid my mini skirt up around my waist, pulled the ribbons on my panties and exposed me completely, then he dropped his pants and shorts and there was that beautiful, huge, throbbing cock. He opened my lips and placed the huge head against my cunt. He leaned over and kissed me and played with my breasts until I asked him to please fuck me hard and fast, or I might change my mind. We came together and he filled me with his cum. Because this was forbidden sex, it was more intense than with you Eric. Stan asked if I wanted to continue and I said yes, Eric won't be home till 9 tonight.

We put ourselves back together and I took him home to our bed. We didn't know what time was and it seemed like we made love forever. The sex was beautiful and he held me and caressed me after each time. He was a romantic at heart and I loved the things he said to me. After our sixth intercourse, he told me this would have to be our last, but only for now. Eric, you told me we were so enraptured with each other that during the sixth time we made love, you actually walked into the hall by our bedroom's open door, and watched our last time, for it was after nine. Stan left me with a long passionate kiss. I could hardly let him go. I was lying naked on the bed, Stan's huge amount of semen back flowing out of me, when you walked in and stripped off your clothes, as you asked if I had a good time.

"I wanted to shout to the world I had his big cock and I had orgasms before, but these were orgasms! He took me like I had never been taken," I thought. There was no way to answer your question fully, so I said softly, "Yes!"

You slipped in to our bed beside me and kissed me and told me you loved me and you'd like details. Eric you asked me to kneel above your head so you could lick my lover's cum from my thoroughly dilated vagina and I told you all Stan and I did, from the classroom to the final. We finished in more ways than one and were lying together facing.

You were prepared for my question, Stan and you had talked as he left and the two of you had already agreed if I wanted it.

"Eric," I said, "I want to be with my Stan again--alone--as soon as possible."

You said, "He'll pick you up here Friday after school and take you to his home for the weekend, and his girl friend Susan or 'Wild Thing' as I came to christen her, would spend the weekend with me, Eric.

We agreed this was what we wanted, and the swap is what happened, for that first weekend and a significant number after.

There were many times we had that threesome we had initially planned, but as the months progressed, you told me you enjoyed watching us two as much as you enjoyed doubling me. You told me I was so beautiful and totally responsive with him. You said you had never seen anyone have the intensity of orgasms with him that I had with him. He seemed to know exactly what I needed and could deliver it. You told me that we were the most perfectly sexually matched couple you had ever seen.

Christmas came and you planned a surprise for me. I bought you an electric train that year, because I kept 'remembering' my child-hood train. You had bought me a sexy lingerie outfit and matching high-high heels. It was pale mist blue. It consisted of a little string ribbon tie sheer jacket falling just below my breasts, the French cut panties were also ribbon tie at the sides, the garter belt and hose were a perfect match to the bra and bikini. I asked you to open your gift first, and you told me it was just what you'd had when you were a boy. Then I opened mine. You asked me to go to our bedroom and put it on and then let you see me by the Christmas tree.

You said Stan had been waiting in our dark kitchen and quickly came out, stark naked with a huge erection from just from hearing my pretty voice and the anticipation of having all of you. You quickly tied six ribbons at two inch intervals, each with a bell on his erect cock. He stood just in the darkness of the kitchen off the dining room where we had the Christmas tree. I came back to the tree and you told me I was a vision of sexual excitement.

You said that you had another gift and came to me and kissed me until Stan could be standing behind me.

We finished the kiss, you quickly moved aside as I opened my eyes and saw Stan.

You said "I'm giving you your lover for Christmas.'"

He stepped to me and took me in his arms and I kissed him and I touched the bells and ribbons and asked, "What are these for? Do they have a purpose?"

You said they do and Stan kissed me as he slipped the ribbons loose on the jacket and took the jacket off exposing my beautiful breasts to his hands and mouth.

You untied the ribbons at the panties sides and my lover, and your fellow 'Hunter' picked me up in your stockings and high heels and carried you to our bed and lay you down.

You told me that you had never seen any woman lubricate and relax so fast, as Stan positioned above me, I placed him for entry and he slid in two inches. You removed a belled ribbon, he went four; we proceeded as you told me at each bell ring, his next 2 inches was another gift from you. When you removed the sixth, you told me how much you loved me, and you said you wanted only the best sexual partner for me. I was with him many times before, but as Stan fully penetrated me with 14 thick inches, you said that we were so beautiful together and I came solely on the gentle slow penetration and your words. You kissed me, told me he was all mine, and I was all his, and to enjoy myself. You said you would be sleeping in the bedroom across the way. I wrapped my stocking covered legs around Stan's back and held him as to receive his last streams of come. You told me that seeing my pretty heels on his back was so erotic.

As we made love, you watched us through the open doors, and you set up your train. You said that seeing the two of us and hearing the sounds of sex and the beautiful sounds of the two of us coming was fantastic. Several hours passed and then there was a long erotic interlude of passionate kissing, and then Stan entered me again and very quickly I was coming so beautifully, when I said, "Stan, I love you."

Eric, two days later when 'Christmas Sex' was over, you talked to me about what you heard, and why it bothered you. At first I said I hadn't said it, and then I confessed I had extreme feelings for Stan, but different than I had for you. You said you thought it would be best if you were always involved when we had sex. I agreed to that verbally, but I never physically implemented it. We had threesomes, but as a couple Stan and I had the greatest joy in sex. Our relationship continued into the fall, when you accepted a job with Mobil in Dallas. While you were away, Stan came to our home many times, and we never stopped until the moving van pulled away when school ended for me.

Being with him honed my skills as a sex partner, and you told me I was impressive before!

You tried to involve me in Texas with some other men but I flatly refused on the basis that I didn't want to get too emotionally involved. In 78, you talked of going to parties and suddenly I showed an interest, but only in fantasy in our bedroom. You told me of fantasies which were actual realities of Janet's parties, and Jennifer's and your parties and I was turned on immensely. Then one day I asked you to tell me about the wildest, raunchiest party you'd ever been to. The way I phrased it, it seemed clear to me you knew I had been telling you reality and these were my actual recollections. I started the story and entered you, and paced myself to the story for its rousing climax and our rousing climaxes. When we were complete, I lay down beside you, and you told me that was a most different experience than you had ever had with Stan or me. A few months later, you started wanting hamburgers at 9 am. I suggested you go to the doctor and you came back and announced you were going to be a mother.

You traveled all over the world and to D.C. and thirty-seven of the fifty states in our 35 years. It was hard on me, for you to be gone so much and it was hard on you too. When you were home you hunted my attractive friends and none of them ever told me except one.

You were on a business trip for two weeks when she decided to tell me that you two had been having sex. I should have known, because you were leading me into fantasies of a threesome with her by name and describing her in accurate detail. I guess you wanted me to confront me. When I found out, the offenses were two, one much more severe than the other.

You had been cheating on me, but more importantly I had been trying to convert her to Christianity and you may have damaged that.

It had been just at two years three months, since our first son was born. You had been having 'that feeling' but you didn't care, you wanted to get even for my being with Judy.

I asked my friend to keep James from noon till 10 pm and I went out in search of 'get even sex.' I checked into a hotel. I found a handsome businessman calling it an early day, then I tried an average guy in the hotel bar and found him lacking-nothing here to say 'see, I got even!' Then I headed for the parking lot to do some scouting elsewhere and I met a handsome black man and invited him to my hotel room. He was packing and was a high repeater, and from first entry I started coming with him! Toward the end of our short session (for he had to go to a business meeting) I came so hard with him and he filled me with his cum for about ten long pulses.

I had 'that feeling' and I knew I was in trouble for I was fertile! My 'get even sex' game had turned deadly serious. I called information, got Stan's number, and he said he would welcome me. When I told him what I'd done, he said everything would be alright. I checked out, rushed home, picked up James and called my mother to tell her I was coming for a visit. I was there in three hours, left James with his grandmother, and said I needed to be gone about three or four hours. It was 7 pm when Stan let me in and took me in his arms. I elected him to make me a mother, and he did. The typing characteristics match. I called you from his house and told you I had rushed up to check on my parents, and would stay till Sunday when you'd be coming home from your business trip. Stan made the most of those three hours and he and I had four to six hour sessions with him for each of the next five days.

# The Perfect Season

Donna, I wish we could go back to that day when I was sitting on the fountain behind the OU Student Union and you came walking up to me in your white short shorts and mid-riff knotted, sky-blue blouse and sat down beside me. You were talking about having Desiree and me over again to eat with you and Rick, so you could try a new, Mexican meal. You were so close to me, I could smell your perfume and I wanted you, and I reached out and gently touched your beautiful leg with my finger tips. Your skin felt so good. You did not pull away, nor did you ask me to stop. We talked about class schedules and it turned out that on M W F we both had the same 3 hours free, right at lunch. The semester had just started and we had met and talked at the fountain a couple of times the first week. Remember, you said you were just heading home for lunch. You asked if I had eaten, and when I said no, you invited me to go home with you. Your house was 5 minutes away.

You told me to sit on the couch in front of the fireplace and we would eat there. Since it was August, the AC was on and perhaps a little too cool. I got up and walked to the breakfast bar and watched you making sandwiches at the cabinet. As I watched, I noticed you really had a great body--beautiful legs, very curved and as you moved and caught

the cold air of the air conditioning
across your blouse, your nipples grew
hard and it became obvious you were
braless. I admired your beauty as you
worked, and then remembering the AC was a
little cold, I asked if I could turn it
up. You told me the thermostat was just
down the hall just before yours and
Rick's room. As I turned it down, I
looked into your room and noted the king
size bed was deeply turned down and ready
for use.

I came back into the den and you were
on the couch and the sandwiches and our
drinks were on the coffee table. As I sat
down beside you, I thought of all my
wife's friends who I had seduced in the
few years we'd been married, and I
thought, what would be wrong with one
more, for I've already done the harm? Our
marriage had not cured my sex addiction
or hunting as I had hoped.

We ate and talked and flirted.
Suddenly, you lifted your pretty bare
legs over mine. I stroked them and your
bare mid-riff, as both of us continued to
flirt--then wanting more, I lifted you up
(how small you were) and pulled you on to
my lap to kiss you, fondle your breasts,
and introduce you to my hardness.

I commented on no bra, and you
teasingly asked me how I knew you had
anything on. It hit me I'd seen no panty
lines in the tight fitting short shorts
when I had checked out your firm cheeks
as I'd followed you to your car to open
the door for you. I paused, thinking for
a moment. Perhaps you thought I was not
committing fast enough. You suggested to
me I was welcome to find out for sure.

Without hesitation, I picked you up in my arms as we laughed, and I carried you to your bedroom and lay you gently on your bed.

First I took your blouse off and exposed your beautiful firm breasts. Your nipples were hard (not from air conditioning but from excitement). They and their areolas were dark pink and quite large for a little girl. Remember how I spent a long time caressing your breasts and kissing you. Perhaps too long, for in a little while you reminded me that I'd brought you in there to determine something. With out hesitation, I unbuttoned and unzipped your shorts and carefully pulled them down over your hips and cleared the zipper over your Mound of Venus, for you were truly naked. I then removed them from your legs, leaving you so pretty.

Sensing you wanted to move right along; I quickly shed my clothing and stood beside the bed, and asked if we needed to do anything. I always asked and complied, but to me, if there is no skin contact, and fluid exchange, then there is no real sex.

You said, "No silly, I want to feel you come in me. You are even better than I imagined!"

With that, I grew even more excited in anticipation of filling you, my cuddly little girl. I remember I started to move between your legs and you had me stop and take the other pillow and place it beneath your round firm cheeks. You said you liked it that way, to get maximum penetration. I think this time, you got more penetration than you expected or had

ever had before. I think every time we
played, we made love three, four, or five
times, then cleaned up together in the
shower, and sometimes played again in
there, and then we headed back to campus.
You beautiful little girl--you were a lot
of fun!

One day, late in the semester, as we
loved each other, I said you were
developing a little bulge in your board-
flat, stomach and that your uterus was
softer when I deeply penetrated you and
accidentally touched it, and your nipples
and areola were enlarging and taking on a
darker color. I was moving in you as I
said it and we were both rapidly
approaching orgasm. Hearing me say that,
Donna you came so hard! Then you returned
to reality just as I began mine.

You said, "Eric you've made me a
mother!"

Talk about men not liking to commit! I
pulled out of you as I was coming. I
streamed across your once flat-belly, and
across your changing breasts and left a
lot of white creamy pearls in your brown
hair. One stream even hit you in the left
eye, occluding it for a time, one of your
grey blue eyes I was always so fond of
looking into when we made love!

Still kneeling over you, my normal
brain returned to half functioning, and I
said, "How?"

I was still fully erect as always, and
I maintained, only with the stimulation
of looking at you. I was slowly
streaming, for I had not finished. You
leaned up, reached out and took hold and
stroked the last creamy cum out of me,
directed it to pool in your little dark

brown fluff of hair, You asked what I
thought my package and creamy liquid was
for?

I laughed and then I collapsed beside
you, stroking you gently, holding you
like I'd never done before, as you
explained that Rick could not father a
child due to a childhood illness, and
would cooperate in no other way, so you
had elected me to be the father of your
child--and had a great time doing it and
wanted me now so much more!"

*Desire Davidson*

# Got a Minute?

I saw her leave the Thai Embassy and cross the street and head toward the park. She was headed right for me. She was a doll. The weather was mild in Hong Kong with just a tinge of coolness. Rachel was wearing a white linen blouse and a red 'Scottish' plaid skirt which ended about six inches above her knees. She was wearing black, high-heeled boots and red stockings. I heard the tap, tap, tap, of her heels on the park sidewalk. I had to act quickly. I headed up the sidewalk and noted she was wearing a watch.

I said, "Got a minute, do you have the time?"

She stopped and said it was 11:33.

I fiddled with my watch and as I did it, I said, "Hi, I'm Eric, you have a beautiful 'Aussie' accent." I paused for her to fill in her name.

"Rachel," she said "Rachel."

"What a lovely name you have, Rachel," I said.

"Rachel", I said, "I just got off my ship--I'm in the U.S. Navy--and have never been here before, so can you tell me a good place to have lunch?"

She said," Yes, I'm headed to a restaurant on the other side of the park; why don't you join me."

I walked with her through the park and found out she was an English teacher specializing in taking one who has learned formal English and teaching them to relax their formal speech and that included their gaining an understanding of idioms and slang of the language."

"It makes the speaker relaxed and more real," she told me.

Rachel and I had lunch and all during lunch, she was asking me about American idioms and American slang usage. She was working with the Thai Ambassador and had been for two weeks getting him ready to meet with the American Ambassador and the British Ambassador. He wanted to fit in instead of sounding like a parrot. Language improvement tutoring was how she made her living.

I asked, "How did you end up in Hong Kong?"

Rachel said, "I followed my fiancée here and I caught him in bed with a Chinese girl young enough to be his daughter, so the planned wedding was off, but I decided to stay anyway."

"At first I taught school," She said, "But soon I found tutoring paid much more and for far less hours."

She continued to ask me about American idioms and slang and I continued to think of them. Rachel said, "You know I have the whole afternoon available. Why don't you come to my apartment and let me tape record your examples."

I was ready and willing--my cock had been hard since I heard the tap, tap, tap of her boots heels. She navigated some 10 blocks and we came to an apartment building. She guided me to her apartment and we set about drinking cokes and recording examples of slang and idioms.

She was beautiful. She had sparkling grey eyes set in a beautiful face framed by lovely black hair flipped under at her shoulders. Her lipstick coordinated with the red of her plaid outfit and made her lips inviting. The red contrasted with the white of her long sleeved blouse which revealed the form of her C-cup breasts. Yes, Rachel was quite beautiful.

"Why don't we take a break?"

For the first time, she sat down in an easy chair across from mine. She must have noticed the bulge in my pants giving her the best compliment of all. I could now see much of her legs as she sat in the chair and they were excellent.

"I'm honored to be in the home of such a beautiful woman," I said.

Before she could protest I stood and covered the short distance between us, and was helping her to her feet. I kissed her and she kissed back.

"Can you stay longer?" she asked.

I answered, "I have a 72 hour liberty and I am at your disposal any time you want me."

She turned her face up to kiss me and our greedy mouths met. I picked her slender frame up and carried her to her bedroom and we lay on the bed for a long time passionately kissing.

Finally, Rachel said, "Will you make love to me, I haven't had anyone in a year and you look like the man I want to end my dry spell."

I kissed her and asked how she wanted me to make love to her.

Rachel said, "Let's start with 'missionary' and see where it leads."

We stood up and undressed each other. She had beautiful breasts crowned with large pink nipples which were very sensitive to the touch of my fingers, lips and tongue. The areolas crinkled and bumped as I ran my tongue around them. She was hard and excited. I touched her pretty mound of dark curly hair and found a wet slit waiting for me.

I placed Rachel on the bed and positioned myself between her legs; she took my cock and nestled the head in her lips. I eased in slowly giving her a chance to accommodate my big cock without any discomfort. When she was fully relaxed she took all of me in her and my big balls were resting on her bottom. I began to move and then accelerated thrusts for my Rachel's pleasure Very soon the beautiful little girl was coming on me in wave after wave of orgasms. After about 15 minutes I joined her and filled her cunt with my sperm laden cum.

We lay together for a long time just looking into each others eyes and enjoying what we beheld. Later we would make passionate love in several positions for my beautiful Rachel was greedy for maximizing her pleasure. I stayed the night and then the other two days and nights I had available. Rachel called the Thai Ambassador's secretary and told her she was ill and Rachel and I had nothing other to do than make loves on those three days!

*Desire Davidson*

# Double Entry Accounting

Stan and I were fellow hunters and had occasionally hunted together when we were young. We were talking one day about my wife being really attracted to him. He said if I gave him permission to seduce Desiree, then I could have his girlfriend, Susan. I agreed. My wife called Susan 'Wild Thing' primarily for her fluffy wild blonde hair style that she had when the four of us were seated together at a school banquet. My cock was hard the whole time I was near her. Her perfume or was it natural pheromone made me want to fuck her right there. A few weeks later I found my wife had correctly tagged her, but for sex--the girl loved it and wanted every thing a man (or men) could give her. Susan was totally open to the idea of entertainment with me and was available the next Saturday afternoon. Coincidentally I would be free, because my wife was going shoe shopping with her sister and her mother.

I went to Stan's house at the appointed time of 1 pm. Stan's car was not in the driveway, but Susan's was. I rang the bell and much to my pleasant surprise Susan opened the door and invited me in. Susan was wearing an open front beige lingerie jacket and matching bikini panties--the sheerness of the material did nothing to hide her beautiful body. The top and bottom had little pale blue ribbon ties. Susan was a doll! At 6' she was only two inches shorter in height than me. She had on bone colored high heels at the time, so actually with the heels and a good six inches of teased hair, she was taller than me. Stan told me she was 25. I was 26 at the time of our first sexual encounter. She would be the 1,750 th sex partner of my life. She was going to be fun. Susan had beautiful long legs and I could already envision them wrapped around my back (with her high heels still on) while I fucked her face to face and looked into her pretty grey eyes. She probably was a true blonde when she was a child; for even now the cover of her mons was very light blonde brown.

Susan invited me to sit down on the sofa. We talked a little while.

She said, "Eric, I work for a credit card company in Accounting. What do you do?"

"Well, I returned to college after a stint with the Navy and I am finishing my degree in Electrical Engineering." I told her.

"She had attended all the school she wanted," she told me.

"When I was through with high school in Oklahoma City I completed my formal education for all time. It's hard to have lots of fun in high school when you have to do so much work," she said.

I said, "I grew up right here in the Tecumseh-Shawnee area."

As we continued to talk, my cock was straining to get out of my pants and her big firm nipples strained equally against the sheer fabric of her top. I thought both of us were adequately acquainted and

I began to softly stroke her soft legs. With my other hand, I touched her warm face and told Susan how beautiful she was. I moved forward and kissed her warm, wet, full lips softly and she kissed back but much more firmly. We continued to kiss as she carried me beyond soft to passionate then to ultra-passionate open mouth kisses. As we kissed I continued to stroke her long ivory legs.

After about 15 minutes I stood up and undressed and turned to face her.

Susan said, "Wow! You're almost as big as Stan and he's huge."

I returned to sit by her and placing a finger to her lips I said, "I think you will find my cock much easier for oral and other activity."

I reached for the little bows holding the top closed and I untied them. This allowed me to feel the soft warm skin of her breasts and to directly fondle her large pink nipples.

"They are lovely," I said. I leaned over and tongued and suckled them.

She said, "That feels great, keep doing it--Stan never pays enough attention to my breasts!"

I did keep doing it after she stood up and let me take the jacket off and then her panties. Then she sat down by me. Now we were nude together.

I said, "Susan, I am about to burst to have you, are you ready for sex?"

"Yes," she said, as she led me to the bedroom.

She lay down and her beautiful, wispy blonde hair covered the pillow.

I was too inflamed to wait. I moved over her. My cock was fully hard and my balls were ready to plant my sperm in this pretty prize.

Susan took my cock in her hand and placed me into her delicious, tight, wet pussy. (It made me wonder how much fore play she had to have with Stan before sex, for he is significantly thicker then I am and he could have never entered her now.)

I moved into her and her cunt felt great. Fully in her, I leaned down and kissed her full firm ivory breasts and flicked her big pink nipples with my tongue, as I built her excitement.

Susan said, "I love the way you make love to my breasts--you're the only man I've been with who does that.  Swirl your tongue around my areola some more."

Susan said, "I'm adjusted to your big cock now and I want to be fucked."

Her pussy was wet and very tight on my cock so I began to take long slow strokes. As she relaxed I sped up the pace of my thrusts in her pretty body. Susan's clit was very prominent and very shortly the classy little girl started coming on me as we continued to fuck. She continued to come in waves and in a few minutes I couldn't hold back and I joined her and shot stream after stream of hot cum into her pretty body. When we had both finished, I pulled out of her and held her and kissed her in the afterglow of a beautiful sexual experience.

About thirty minutes had elapsed since we started. I asked her to '69' with me. She was a great cock sucker and from the hard loud orgasms, I believe I was proving I knew my way around her delicious cunt. I came in her mouth and I

moved up and in a deep kiss, Susan gave
my cum back to me. We continued to touch,
fondle and kiss for a long time. Then I
asked Susan what sex position she would
like to try.

Susan said, "I occasionally like anal
sex, but Stan is so big I won't let him
touch me that way. You're big but not so
huge in thickness--I'd like to take you
that way. "

We kissed and fondled for several more
minutes, then I prepared her for entry.

I reached for my zippered pouch and
got out lubricant for our next romp. I
prepared her by opening her anus with my
three lubricated fingers until I was sure
she could take me comfortably. Then she
lubricated my long hard cock. Her hands
felt wonderful as she coated me and then
briefly jacked me off.

Susan lay on her back and I took her
beautiful long legs over my shoulders. I
took my cock in my hand while supporting
my weight on one arm and placed the
swollen purple head against her relaxed
anus. I gently moved in and slowly
pressed past her sphincter muscle and
completely entered her body to the full
length of my cock.

Susan, "Are you comfortable?" I said.

"Eric go ahead, I'm adjusted to your
cock and it feels wonderful so deep in my
ass."

I picked up the pace and in a short
order my lovely long legged nymph was
milking huge streams of cum out of my
cock and balls.

Susan did not come with anal
intercourse, so when we finished I lay
between her long legs and tongued her

clit. Shortly she was crying out in ecstasy as waves of orgasms swept over her body.

I went to the bath room and cleaned up, and returned with a warm washcloth to remove the lubricant that remained on Susan.

On my return, I had her kneel over my face with my head supported on a doubled pillow. I bathed her clit in licks and very shortly she was writhing as she came repeatedly to my flicking tongue. Susan finally satiated herself and moved off and lay down beside me. We both needed a break and we just lay for a long time just looking at each other. As a couple we fucked one more time in the face to face position. Almost two hours had elapsed when we heard Stan come in the front door.

I called out, "Did you come to watch?"

Stan replied, "I'd love to but I need your help. I'd like to watch as a participant."

He went on to say Susan had never been double penetrated (ass and cunt) by two men. "I thought we could change that while you're here." he said.

Susan wanted to try it also. We went about the logistics of it. I would lie on my back and facing toward my feet, Susan would impale her body on my cock. Stan would then lay her back on my body and then as I held her, he would enter her pussy. That is exactly what happened and the result proved exactly what I had experienced in the past with other woman, Susan came so heard her cries of passion proved that she was "Wild Thing." She was a delicious fuck and she really came

unglued when Stan began to come in her
cunt and then I joined in her ass--she
was amazing--what a delicious sex
partner!

Stan did seduce my wife Desiree, and I
was alone with his beautiful Susan some
21 other times.

*Desire Davidson*

# What a Woman Wants

Elizabeth wore a gray knee-length wool skirt, cream-colored blouse and pale pink cardigan and had her long, curly blond hair drawn up in a loose cluster of curls and appeared calm and composed as she stood in my hotel doorway.

I was wearing a towel because I had just come out of the shower. Seeing her instantly made me hard and I was having a tough time hiding it.

Elizabeth said, "I wanted to come over and ask you a few questions before we go to dinner. You said I should learn to leave work behind and use dinners to socialize and make alliances."

I had recruited Elizabeth at SMU. She was the brightest engineer I had ever recruited, she had a perfect 4.0 and graduated with honors, but best of all she was gorgeous! I had also recruited Henry Chan who was turning out to be a less than stellar engineer, even though he had the same academic credentials as Elizabeth--she just tried harder. Right after I finished calling my wife, Henry called my room and told me he was going to skip dinner. (He made a bad decision-- I would be cutting him when we returned to Dallas) Then I went to the shower.

I was just getting out of the shower and I wrapped a towel around me and went to the door.

Elizabeth was 22 and I was 30. She was a 'pup' engineer and due to my mentors Carl and John, I was carrying around fifty years of practical engineering knowledge in my head. It would be my job to pour that into Elizabeth as we worked together.

I stayed in my towel and Elizabeth and I sat down in the two chairs in the hotel room. I couldn't get my erection to go down and I was sure she could see the big bulge. Oh, well maybe she would take it as a compliment. Elizabeth asked her questions and I answered and she absorbed the information like a sponge soaking up water. After that she asked if she could stay while I dressed, because she was already ready and it would be more convenient. I protested and then I relented.

I walked toward the dressing nook after telling her to switch chairs so I could have some privacy. I ignored her presence and toweled off my legs, ass and my still erect cock. I selected some light blue bikini underwear (hardly enough to hold my cock); tan socks, kaki pants and a light blue Polo shirt. I retrieved my belt and loaded my pockets with the essentials of life. As I stepped into my brown loafers, I told Elizabeth I was ready and she joined me at the door.

In 1980, Midland, Texas had some great restaurants due to the oil boom economy. I had chosen an up-scale but relaxed dress code restaurant for the evening. I thought Elizabeth would like it after spending the day in jeans, shirt, work boots, and hard hat.

When we were being seated I could see heads turning in the room--yes, she was that beautiful and she was with me,

We looked at the menu and Elizabeth said, "They have Escargot for appetizers--have you ever eaten them?"

I told her no, stuffed mushrooms were on my mind, however for you I will try anything you want. I ordered for the two of us just like we were on a date--we had escargot for the appetizer and each of us had rib eye steak and sautéed shrimp in garlic butter. Elizabeth teased me when I immediately ate three of the escargots. She said you must have had them before. I assured her I was a virgin in that one area, but I had found in my life that when the opportunity for a new adventure presents itself, then seize it!

The meal was great and the company was best--what more could you want--well I wanted Elizabeth!

As we drove into the parking space at the hotel, Elizabeth asked if questions were permitted after dinner--could she come in and talk awhile. I told her she could, and shortly I opened my room for her.

She asked if she could use my bathroom and I said I hope you don't mind the mess. When she came back, I went myself and then walked out into a world of opportunity. Elizabeth was lying on the bed and inviting me to lie down and face her so we could talk. I answered the opportunity. As I lay down, I noticed she had taken the pink sweater off. The imprint of hard nipples was exposed through her cream colored blouse. Her grey skirt had a generous slit in it and it was open showing an ample amount of her beautiful legs. If things went well, I was going to enjoy this conversation.

Elizabeth asked three questions. One about metering crude oil, one about sampling crude oil, and one about why did I find her so attractive.

I replied, "Little Doll, I have not been with many women as gorgeous as you, but that's not why I can't take my eyes off of you--it's because you're both gorgeous and have a beautiful mind that knows no limits."

I reached over and began to unbutton her blouse and when free I reached into her bra and fondled her special firm C-cup breasts. She neither protested nor encouraged. I pushed her onto her back and kissed her passionately for a very long time. Then I returned to her bra--it was a front close model and I opened it and freed her firm young breasts. In keeping with equity I swirled my tongue over each of her luscious pink nipples--tasting each and then returning to her full mouth. I ended a deep kiss and without hesitation, Elizabeth asked, "Do you want to fuck me? I put my diaphragm in."

I told her I wanted her more then than I'd wanted anyone in a very long time. She stood up and let her pretty clothes fall to the floor and returned to the bed now completely naked. I pulled my Polo shirt over my head and dropped everything to the floor and joined her. As I kissed her, I pushed her onto her back and proceed to kiss her pretty flesh all over ultimately alighting on her cunt. I began to lick her clit and she came like an explosion and kept on coming. I stayed with her for several minutes and then positioned us for face to face entry.

Just as I was entering her, the little scamp said "I have a question about gauging cocks."

For that, I punished her by ramming my big cock into her to the hilt in one stroke. In a very few strokes my pretty blond baby was coming again. I continued for several minutes and then I joined her as I shot stream after stream of cum into her body. We were overcome by the passion and excitement and we just kept on fucking. For sex, honor, and love, without constraints and a question from Elizabeth.

*Desire Davidson*

# Come With Me

It was a nice restaurant in the old part of Austin, Texas which at the time had become quite chic.

The couple had been seated just after I was seated. I had already noticed her in the waiting area. She was a beautiful blonde, slim with a firm beautiful ass and full C-cups. She was wearing a short yellow dress with spaghetti straps-- almost a sun dress--the weather was un- seasonably warm. She had on light green high heels and no stockings were visible. She looked to be about 28. She had a pretty tan. He was dressed in casual clothes, slacks and a polo shirt and brown loafers. By chance, they were seated at a table angled just so I could see them both. I guessed they were married to each other from their rings and how they responded to each other. There appeared to be an element of hostility between them.

I was dressed much like the man except my shirt was blue instead of green. I was out looking for a meal, but I was also looking for a filling dessert of a beautiful woman to make love to.

The thought came to mind I had never tried getting a woman to follow me away from her husband. The more I thought about it, the more I liked the risk and I selected it as my sexual adventure for the evening.

The rib eye steak I ordered and the 'fixins' were delivered in short order. The couple I was interested in was having salad and smaller cut steaks. I hurried through my meal and ordered coffee and paid the bill. I watched the couple the whole time I ate classifying them for a proper approach in this new adventure. Of the pair the woman was dominate. In my mind I was already making her mine.

The couple was within five minutes of finishing their meal when I went over to the beautiful blonde and whispered in her ear, "Leave him for tonight--teach him a lesson for what he's done, you're too beautiful for him, come with me and I will give you a sexual experience you'll never forget. Now get up and tell him you're going with me and I'll bring you home in four hours; you will be perfectly safe."

The blonde got up and whispered to him exactly what I had told her and then she walked out hand-in-hand with me. Her husband never moved and sat there stunned.

I put her in my car and drove to my hotel. She was laughing in the excitement of actually doing what I told her and it working. I was pretty pleased too, I had her.

I'm Janelle," she said, "I never dreamed I would go with a man who asked me on the spur of the moment."

As we parked I asked her if she was sure she wanted to have sex with me. She confirmed she was. I leaned over and kissed her gently and then we kissed with more passion.

"Let's go," she said.

I opened my door and went around the car and opened Janelle's door and caught a glimpse of her beautiful legs. I took her hand and led her to my room.

My hotel had turn down service so the bed had already been turned down. The room was large enough to have a small love seat and one wing back chair. I directed her to the love seat and we began kissing and I fondled her breasts through the sheer fabric of her dress. Her nipples were large and easily excited. The feel of her lightly tanned satin smooth legs was wonderful.

I walked to the bed and took the two chocolates the maid had left on the pillow and returned to the love seat. I gave her a chocolate from my pillow and asked her if she would show me her charms for a chocolate.

"Give me both of them," she teased, "and I will give you me!"

We struck a deal as I handed over the second chocolate.

Janelle stood up and un-zipped her dress and let it fall to the floor. She stood before me with bare breasts, panties and high heels.

I said, "You can take the panties off but I want you to keep your pretty high heels on."

In the soft lamp light I could see that although her mons was closely cropped, my pretty baby was a natural blonde.

She came to me and I took her in my arms and kissed her several times. For the third time I asked her if she was sure she wanted to make love with me.

"Yes, I want you," she replied.

I placed her on the bed. She watched as I removed my clothes. When I was fully naked I could no longer conceal my big cock. It was throbbing against my flat

belly and ready to have this lovely
dessert. Janelle took me in her hand as I
stood by the bed and then she invited me
to fuck her. I moved between her legs and
with one finger, then two, then three in
her wet cunt. I determined she was ready
and relaxed. She took my cock in her hand
and guided me into her cunt. What a
marvelous cunt she had, she tightened her
muscles and it was obvious she knew her
technique well. I moved completely into
her and allowed her to get accustomed to
my size and then we began a twenty minute
fuck. Janelle was highly orgasmic and
she came for several minutes as she cried
out, "Oh God! you feel so good…that's it
keep fucking me harder!"

Eventually I could not resist having
my dessert and as I cried out in ecstasy
I shot streams of creamy cum into her.
When we finished, I immediately moved
into a 69 position so she could lick my
cock and I could lick my cum out of her
pussy and tongue her pink clit. This
brought us to beautiful simultaneous
orgasms. Then we lay in each others arms.

We lay resting for a time but
continued to touch faces, lips, breasts
and cock and cunt as we enjoyed just
being with each other. Janelle told me
her favorite position was woman astride
and she would like to do that with me. I
said that would be wonderful. Then I
noted the time and realized we had been
having our private party for three hours
since we left the restaurant. I asked
Janelle how long it would take to get to
her place--she said they lived out by the
lake; so it would take an hour to get
there. I told her to call her husband and

tell him she was having such a great time
she had decided to spend the night. I
laughed as the horny little nymph came
back into my arms. I asked her what he
said--all he said was I'll expect you in
the morning.

Janelle, my special sexual adventure,
continued into the early morning.
Eventually she slept. I held her as she
went to sleep. I did not sleep, for when
I feel like I felt that night I never
need sleep and I never get tired and with
a continual adrenal rush my body goes
sexually for days. In the early sunrise,
she stirred awake and she called me back
into her body for another session of
beautiful sex. Janelle was a living doll
who liked every thing I liked. I did take
her home and her husband was already gone
for the day, so we made love one last
time in her own bed.

# The Best Cure for Jet Lag

Our plane was an L1011 with a center
section of five seats and two seats on
each side of the plane. I was seated in
the center section in the right-most
seat, and this center section faced the
bulkhead. Only one other seat was
occupied in my center row so far--a young
black man was sitting in the left-most
seat. There were three seats between us
and I was hoping to raise the arms and
stretch out in the four seats and sleep
the flight away.

Down the aisle came an attractive
young lady dressed in a soft green
jogging suit. Her long brown hair
cascaded on to the shoulders of her suit.
Her seat assignment was next to mine and
I stood up and helped her get her large
carry-on-bag into the overhead bin. Then
I sat down and found her beside me.

"Hi, I'm Eric," I said.

She replied, "I'm Danni."

The flight attendant came on making
announcements; she had a California
accent which I liked; it was good to be
going home. It was hard though to leave
my wife and two young boys in Oklahoma
for a week after Christmas.

The announcements were over and
everyone was buckled up and shortly we
were in the air.

"Danni are you going home?" I asked.

"Yes," she said, "I visited my parents in Dallas for Christmas." She asked if I was going home.

"Yes," I replied, "My wife and boys are coming home next week so I'll be at loose ends for awhile."

Danni told me she lived in Ontario.

"I flew out of the airport there since I couldn't get flights out of LA. My car is waiting for me there," I told her.

Danni and I talked during the flight.

She said, "I'm 23 and I'm getting married on Valentines Day.

I said, "Your wedding day will be the day after my birthday, I will be 32."

Near the end of the flight Danni said, "My fiancée is going to meet me at the airport, you'll have to let me introduce you."

Danni was attractive, bright, amusing, and quick witted--in short she was very likeable. We got along very well and our visiting made the flight pass in a moment. We arrived about midnight and I carried her carry-on-bag to the checked baggage carousal to collect her other three bags and my one.

Danni was ready to leave but there was no fiancée! She called his apartment several times and there was no answer. So I waited with her, for the airport was almost deserted, since we were the last arrival for the evening, and I didn't like the looks of some of the last few people who remained. I told her I didn't think David was coming.

After about 30 minutes, I said, "Let me take you home."

Her apartment was only about 25 minutes out of my way and no one was waiting for me.

Danni agreed.

"I said. I'll get a cart for your three big bags, your carry-on and my one bag and briefcase."

We went to my car and filled up the trunk and back seat with bags. I opened the passenger door and seated her, and then I got in the car and drove away. She gave me very clear instructions on how to get from the airport to her apartment and we got there in about 20 minutes instead of the 25 minutes I had estimated.

Danni was a small young woman and she had packed too much, so I helped her get her bags into her apartment.

After getting the bags in, Danni said, "Why don't you stay for some hot chocolate?"

I said, "I'd love to."

Danni said, "Please sit down in the living room on my new love seat."

She made the hot chocolate and then joined me on the love seat. We talked as we sipped our hot chocolate and we got to know each other better. Danni filled my cup up again and that added an extra half hour to my four hour stay with Danni on the airplane, the airport, the drive and now in her apartment.

I said, "Did you buy your wedding dress while in Dallas?"

She replied, "I bought my entire trousseau."

That explained the heavy bags.

She said, "Let me show you my wedding dress."

She took me to her bedroom to help her with the bags. She got the dress out and also laid out her wedding night gown ensemble. She had me turn my back while she took her jogging suit off and put on the bridal dress. She was still zipping it up when she asked me to turn around and help her zip it all the way up. It was a strapless design and was quite beautiful on her. Her bare back and the skin of her breasts exposed by the low cut front were very attractive. I told her that it was lovely and she was beautiful in it.

After she modeled it for awhile, I unzipped her when she was ready and she took it off, and this time I did not turn around! When she laid the dress on the bed she turned around and had only her panties on. Her breasts were beautiful firm C-cups and she had medium size brown nipples with large brown areolas. Danni was not shocked and did not try to hide anything.

She said, "I hoped you would look. Let me hang this dress up and I'm going to reward you for taking such good care of me on my trip."

I took off my clothes and was naked when she turned around from hanging the dress up. "My God! You're big!" she said, as she took off her panties.

I went to her and took her in my arms and kissed her as I felt her small hand begin to stroke my cock.

"Danni" I said, "I think you should have a memory of this you can have when your David is with you on your wedding night."

She looked puzzled at first, but when I picked up the sheer white outfit and separated the negligee from the gown and laid the gown on the suit cases she began to see. I took the sheer negligee and dressed her in it. I turned down the bed and when she was ready I picked up the 'Bride' and carried her to her bed. I placed her on the bed so the negligee was under her and I opened it and spread it out on each side of her. I had made her a pseudo marriage bed of it.

"You remember this," I said, "when David is your partner!"

Then I moved between her legs and leaned over her and kissed her warm, full lips and spent some time with her delightful breasts--so young and firm. I took her nipples into my mouth and brought them fully erect with my tongue. Shortly she was relaxed enough and wet enough to take me. Danni took my cock in her hand and guided me into her. Her cunt was fantastic, for it was just the right tightness on my big cock not to be uncomfortable for her and it was very stimulating for me. I slowly made love to her and in a few minutes I was giving her long hard thrusts.

Danni began to come on my cock, and was a little tigress in her cries and actions as I continued to fuck her. After about twenty minutes, I began to come in the pretty 'Bride'. I quite literally emptied my balls into her. The naughty little bitch deserved every stream of cum that she got. Danni was marvelous.

I pulled out of her still mostly erect and she went down on me and made me come again.

Danni asked, "Please spend the night with me."

I didn't need to be anyplace, so I spent the night with her. It was more than memorable, for she took me several ways, before we fell asleep. Then in the morning light, we started fucking all over again.

*Desire Davidson*

# Variations on a Theme

Andrew had sandy blond hair and was 31 years old while his partner Arthur was 29 and had sun bleached brown hair. They were obviously a couple as I observed them on the beach in Manhattan Beach, California.

Picking up a gay couple is just like picking up a heterosexual couple. I observe which one is making the most decisions and that is the one I approach with the idea of them taking me into their bed.

At age 31 I had become quite adept at picking up both hetro and gay and bisexual couples. I had been bisexual from the very beginning of my sexual career and occasionally went to the other side for a change of pace.

I made my seductive approach on Andrew the dominate one of the pair and Arthur went along for the fun.

They took me to their beach front apartment and we quickly shed our swimming trunks and evaluated assets. Andrew had a thin 6" cock and Arthur had a medium thickness 7" cock. My monster dwarfed both of them put together.

I felt like getting fucked and sucked at the same time, so I put my legs up over Andrew's shoulders and he easily entered my lubricated ass. The position elevated him away from me so the space allowed Arthur to lay his head on my upper belly and take the head of my cock into his mouth. Andrew was thin but he had a just right angle to be stroking my prostate gland with each thrust and I was getting turned on fast from it and Arthur's expert oral attention to my cock. I felt Andrew beginning to come, so I joined him and came in Arthur's mouth; so much that he lost a good portion of cum on my belly. Andrew dismounted and came and licked the cum off my belly and that brought me to full hardness.

I prepared both their asses with lubricant and they had the fun of taking turns fucking each other while I watched and this allowed them to become relaxed enough to take my cock. Each one came in the other.

When they were re-lubricated the two of them lubricated my cock. It felt great to have their four hands stroking my cock. I positioned Andrew on his hands and knees and I entered his ass first. He had a tight little ass and it felt great to my cock. I could feel my glans slide over his prostate with every thrust and soon he was shooting cum all over the king size bed. After he was finished, I came in his ass flooding it with cum.

With a short recovery time, I moved to Arthur. Arthur had a bigger cock and I lay him on his back and took his legs over my shoulders. He was already on fire from having watched me take his partner. I fucked him for about five minutes before he began to shoot cum all over his belly and chest. I joined him and shot stream after stream of cum up his ass.

The apartment door opened and in walked an attractive girl with her brown hair up in a pony tail. Anne was bisexual and rented the second bedroom from the gay couple. As soon as she saw my cock she asked if she could play too. I went to her and took her in my arms and kissed her and told her I wanted to fuck her while the guys watched. The party kept on for another hour and it was about the time I needed to go. Anne was an inconvenient distraction for I could have used her time to make love again with my new gay friends.

For one last parting shot, we four lay on our sides in folded, spoons position, and I entered Anne's pussy, Andrew entered my ass and Arthur entered Andrew's ass and the four of us had sex together. With Andrew stimulating my prostate gland as he fucked me, I flooded Anne's pussy with cum.

I saw the three of them on the beach later in the week (while I was hunting a new partner) and the three friends were complaining that my big cock had left them sore, but they were ready to do it again any time I wanted them.

# The Long Drive Home

Samantha and Gerald were finishing their meal in the 'Sutton County Steak House' in Ozona, Texas as I was finishing mine. I was seated where I could see them all the time and they seemed to be exchanging glances and looking at me and then talking.

They were dressed up. She was wearing an expensive chic green wrap around dress, and sexy spike high heels. He was wearing a western cut suit, had a $3,000 Stetson cowboy hat lying on the chair beside him and had a pair of $5,000 cowboy boots on. They were richly dressed for a Monday night,

I was on my way to visit my technicians in Ft. Stockton after I visited my men here in Ozona. Ozona was a nice little town. The first time I came here one of my Techs told me one man owned almost everything around here. I was about to meet the man.

Gerald got up and came over to my table and asked to set down. He spoke quietly and after introducing himself he asked if I thought he had a beautiful wife in Samantha. I said I thought she was more than beautiful; she is my dream women if I were looking for a sex partner. I had been through this drill a number of times--I was being screened by the husband to share his much younger wife, and I was cutting to the chase.

He made his decision and returned to their table and brought Samantha back with him. She sat across from me.

He introduced his wife and I said, "Samantha I very much want to make love to you."

Samantha said, "I like your looks and want you as a partner, but can you be very discrete and do the kind of things I need done?"

I replied, when I leave your bed there will never be a word said about our love making for the next twenty years and by then it just won't matter." The key thing is I will do what ever you want me to do and I will give you freedom...

Gerald interrupted me and said, "You are perfect for our needs. We live five miles from here will you follow us to our home?"

I followed him down the highway a mile and then turned on to a private road that was better than the best two-lane highway in Texas. When we arrived at the house it was walled and gated. Once inside the mansion courtyard there was a circular drive. Their mansion equaled any grand mansion in Dallas or Houston.

Gerald pulled his silver Mercedes into one of the five garages and the couple came to meet me and we went in together. We didn't stop downstairs; we went straight up stairs to the master bedroom and without ceremony, Samantha and I undressed for play time.

Gerald told me he for the most part liked to watch his wife with new men of her choosing. He said he wanted to just sit and watch me take his wife for the first time.

Samantha was a doll, she was beautiful in body, mind, and spirit as I learned a little about her as we lay on the bed and talked, fondled, and exchanged soft as well as passionate kisses.

Samantha said, "My heart, soul, and spirit are yours tonight. Will you care for me and lead me to the end?"

I thought that was rather cryptic, but I agreed I would do those very things. She had a beautiful 29 year old body and I classed her as a 'Hard Body'--just wonderful to make love to.

Samantha told me she was ready. She wanted face to face and I asked Gerald to come over and place my cock in his wife's cunt. He did it readily and I suspected he was bisexual--we would see. Samantha's cunt was warm, wet and relaxed and my big cock entered her relatively easily. I began to move into Samantha and shortly was giving her maximum stroke length. The pretty baby began to come and as the intensity of orgasms increased I noticed a slight shuddering of her body and a defocused look in her eyes…I had seen this before and I knew I had been selected to be the last.

Samantha cried out in the joy of intense orgasm and I came in her with stream after stream of cum. It was like her pretty body was milking it out of me.

When we finished, Samantha went to the bathroom and I moved over to the wing chair next to Gerald. He was holding a magazine which had stories of sexual encounters. He called my attention to one story in particular and asked if I had ever done that.

"Yes I have done it several times." I said.

"Is it dangerous," he asked.

I said, "It can be deadly, because there is a sharp line separating pleasure of orgasm from chocking to death."

He said, "After you make love to Samantha a few more times I want you to do it to her. Samantha and I have agreed to ask the man we chose tonight to do it for us."

I said, "I will do it for Samantha—I recognize her need."

Samantha and I did make love several ways orally and when she was ready to make love face to face again, I asked if this was the time she wanted her 'freedom.' She was holding my hand and it tremored and I knew she wanted freedom beyond the captivity of her failing body.

I asked, "Am I correct you have a cancerous brain tumor and it is Stage 5-death in six months?"

"Yes." she said.

She kissed me and said, "I can't face the destruction of my life as the cancer takes me. I want to go now—tonight—and have my 'freedom.'"

"Will it hurt?" Samantha asked.

I held her and I said, "There will be no pain; you will go out in an ecstasy of orgasms, and it is my privilege to help you escape the coming disability and pain of your illness.

I lay beside her and told her I would love her and cry tonight for her leaving this world, but someday I would see her again in eternity.

I said, "Is there any last thing you want to do before we start?"

She kissed her husband goodbye and thanked him for letting her avoid a painful death. He was quietly crying as she came back to the bed. I explained what I would be doing and explained the 'stop signal' to use if she changed her mind--it was simply to touch either of my arms.

She lay on her back and I moved over her and she took my cock and guided me into her. As before, she began to come very quickly and I moved one hand to her throat and then a second and began to stop her air supply--her orgasms were ten times stronger than the first. She touched my arm and I release the pressure enough for her to whisper.

"Eric, thank you, please do it now!" Samantha said.

I returned to full pressure and without leaving an earthly mark on her beautiful neck, her eyes lost their light and her spirit stepped into eternity. I had come as she died. I moved off of her and pulled her to me and held her as I cried for her. Gerald came over and said, it's all right, she was very ill. Gerald and I placed her back in bed in a sleeping position.

I asked, "What will come of this?"

Gerald said, "Nothing--I own every thing around here including the city and county officials. Every one knows she was terminally ill."

I dressed and he walked me to the door.

He said, "Thank you for giving her so much pleasure in the last few hours of her life."

He shook my hand and I went to my car and the big ornamental gates opened and allowed me to leave.

It is hard to lose a man, but it is harder to lose a woman in this strange life. But now at least Samantha has her 'freedom'. I have always remembered them with joy and rejoiced in being in the right place at the right time to perform this act of service.

*Desire Davidson*

# A Black and White Fever

Ann, you were a delight, every time I saw you--at the grocery store picking up a few things on the way home, at events at the elementary school where both our children went, and around the stores in the village square. My Bride knew you, and if we were together, and you waved your little flirtatious wave, then she thought noting of it. Sometimes we would meet and talk, so it wasn't like we didn't know each other--after all we lived in the same pine forest north of Houston. You were a flirt, a scamp, a tease--and you were in my forest and very quickly became this hunter's deer--and with all that, you were intelligent, well spoken, dedicated to the school, your church, and gorgeous!

Eric, I agree I was a scamp, but it was your fault I was a flirt and a tease, for I only was when you got near me; it wasn't that I just wanted to 'jump you,' but I was awfully curious about a man who's wife never at any time said anything bad about him, and, in fact praised you! You were just too good to be true--and that made you terribly attractive to me.

Ann, I remember one Saturday, I was in the Village Square running errands for Desiree, and you were there as well, and both of us were childless--what were the odds of that with my three boys and your three girls. We nearly matched in age and

having our children later, they were of
similar age. It was already a Houston
summer even though we'd hardly left
spring. You had your long brown hair in a
pony tail and pulled back through a light
emerald green ball cap, tight, light
emerald green shorts (cut a bit high on
leg and cheek--I wondered if you'd
altered them for effect, for I knew you
sewed), cute, white, seductive sandals,
and a thin low cut, collarless, white
blouse and nothing else, and as we
talked, you unbuttoned a few more buttons
(tease!) on your blouse.

I suggested that we go in the '50's-
Look-Ice Cream Parlor' and have something
to cool off, and you led me in to the
most isolated booth in the back. I
intended to hunt you and you had already
given clear indication you weren't going
to run away on first approach, so we were
actually well along in the clearing of
constraints. We ordered and the place was
almost empty after we were served.

Eric, when we met, I thought what
luck! I would have followed you anywhere
that day, and I even made a thinly veiled
suggestion when we had been alone with
our drinks for awhile. You acted like you
didn't even hear it and moved on. I was a
bit miffed, I had been rejected, although
gently. My emerald green eyes became
quite moist, and you reached over the
table to me and used your handkerchief to
dry the few tears. You told me it takes
time, everything is better with time. I
knew there would be no seduction this
day. There was much of you learning about
me, cautioning me about some of the
feelings I had expressed earlier, and

always that horrible phrase of yours--
'Ann, you have to be sure!' You warned me
several times about being sure. In the
end I was sure--I was the elect--but not
fulfilled. You said, at the right time we
will meet in the 'forest.'

Eric, I can't claim purity before
marriage, or fidelity with my husband--he
was gone a lot as an international
airline pilot. I had needs, but three
girls and my visibility in the community
made it difficult to fulfill them all
when Brad was away for so long. A
'forest' you told me, and I remembered
the time on the jogging trail, when I had
led a hunk of a man into the forest and
gave myself to him. There would never be
a bed of pine needles again--unless the
guy was irresistible, like you!

Ann, we met several other times. You
lived on the third cul-de-sac over from
mine, and I would occasionally jog that
way. One day I jogged your way and
decided to ring your door bell. I had met
your husband at a school function, so it
would be no big deal if he answered. He
did not, you did and the girls were
staying at friends for five hours that
evening. You were going to a women's
auxiliary function at church and you were
getting ready in peace. You quickly told
me you didn't have to go; you were just
one of the officers and you had about
four hours before you had to pick the
girls up. I only had two hours, and if
the times could be combined for six
hours, it would not have been enough to
cherish you.

Eric, I asked you in, and we had a
quick exchange of information and you

asked to stay awhile, and I did cancel my plans. I invited you upstairs to talk to me while I changed to something else--I was thinking quickie--but you were thinking properly cherished for eternity. I gave you cause for the names you've called me. I was dressed up and when I removed my dress, you were very visible in your jogging shorts and were rock hard. I had checked you out every time we'd met and you always gave me the nicest compliment any man could, by responding to my beauty. I wanted to see close up. You got up and walked to me and kissed me very gently to see what I would do, and then started kissing me most passionately. My beautiful body was available to you, but your hands and fingers were on my hair and face, but I had glued myself to your body.

You stepped back and said, "Ann, you have not run, you are committed, and I want to make you mine--but not now--there is not time to properly cherish you so I will always remember you. We could play like teenagers for a while, though!"

I agreed I would like that, and you removed my high heels, my stockings and my lingerie, all the while praising and kissing my body. Then you removed your jogging shoes and clothing, and we stood apart looking at each other. I'd never seen anyone like you.

Eric you turned down the cover of my bed as I watched. Then you picked me up, carried me over and lay me gently down on my bed, and joined me. There was a lot of talk about the two of us, but for the most part it was a fantastic make out session, hotter than I'd ever had when I was young, with the hottest boy I ever had. There was no intercourse and you only let me get you off once, when I told you we were trying to have another baby-- hopefully a boy for my husband. You let me stroke and tongue for it was all I could do--it made me realize how small my hands looked on you and how small my mouth was. You on the other hand taught me what you could do with my large firm breasts. You actually looked to see if I had implants--I saw you but I didn't tease you about it. Besides I had nipple sensitivity to the edge of being orgasmic to the right tongue, and yours was it. You went down on me and kept me coming for most of the last hour of our make- out-session. When I was fully dressed, you did lie back on my bed for a 20 minute hand session and at the end you soaked my hand and wrist and spurted far beyond many times, spotting sheets and carpet."

Ann, I hated to leave you, but I had promised Desiree, I'd be there. I told you the time would come for us to meet in the 'beautiful forest' where time seems to stand still. I actually thought my pretty target was going to be a 'new pregnant mommy-to-be' in a short time, and I admit I moved you to next year in my mental to-do-list.

About two months later, after work I stopped to pick up some items from the store. My timing in getting to the store was very regular at that time in my life, for my professional life had entered what turned out to be a very short lull. The little travel and regularity of schedule for my family was good, but the lack of

adventure was killing me. You came
running to me like you were looking for
me and said you needed my help--right
now, that you had done something really
stupid! I said ok and you led me out to
my company car--I think you had spotted
it there and that's why you came to me. I
put you in and got in myself and you
started to talk a mile a minute about
what you had done and why you had come
for me. What had you done, Ann?

Eric, I had gone off birth control
pills to try for a new baby boy. My
husband was taking longer and longer
flight schedules and he wasn't meeting my
needs in fatherhood or lover or rake. He
was supposed to be home that day, and I
was supposed to pick him up at the
airport, but he called me and told me
they needed a Pilot out of LaGuardia for
a three leg extension. I was so
disappointed because he had been away so
long, and I was also at my most fertile
time. This was supposed to be the night
to make a baby boy. Brad went on and said
since I was going to come out to pick him
up anyway, could I pick up Devon instead.
I asked why and he told me he had called
his wife from New York, and she had told
him in no uncertain terms to not come
home--she was through with his
womanizing. Brad had been telling me over
the several months he'd been flying with
Devon as Co-Pilot, that he was the
biggest womanizer he'd ever seen, and
rumor had it among the flight attendants
that he had the equipment for it and knew
how to use it."

I went to Houston Intercontinental and
picked Devon up. He and his white wife

and their young child went to my church--
so I knew him on sight. Growing up in
Alabama, I'd never even considered a back
man before--the locals would have lynched
both of us! As we drove back to The
Woodlands, he told me to drop him off at
the motel, because he couldn't go home,
but he hoped to talk to his wife,
Rebecca, and heal their split. He told me
he didn't have to fly for 5 days and he
would just stay there if they couldn't
heal. He presented his story like a
wounded little boy, and that was the
first mistake in my thinking. I really
felt sorry for him, and felt if we talked
more about their situation, that I could
give him some very good advice on
renewing their marriage--after all I was
a licensed marriage counselor before my
girls came along.

I had actually been walking on the
forest trails when the call came and
since Brad wasn't coming home, I really
didn't feel like dressing up to pick up
his Co-Pilot.

I had on a pleated sky blue skirt just
like a short tennis skirt that really
showed off my legs, matching cotton
panties, white walking shoes, sky blue
puff-ball socks, and a button-down-the-
front, white, cotton, eyelet, sleeveless
blouse, and no bra--I didn't need it
because I was so naturally firm--'53
Cadillac bumpers' was what my husband
lovingly called them, oddly enough '53
was my year of birth.

As I'd walked the trail in the forest,
I thought of you, and wondered when you
would be back. I was ready now, whenever
you met me this time I was prepared. I

went no where without my diaphragm and spermicidal jelly. I know you are going to laugh, but I thought this would be a good afternoon to see if I could catch you Eric and consummate; my mother had come to be with the girls--I never dreamed how important it might be to be prepared for you, but just in case, before I left to go to the airport, I placed my diaphragm. I had a couple of guys--well four--since our petting session and the diaphragm had worked perfectly."

Eric as we headed north on I-45, I began to talk to Devon about some things to consider as he talked to his wife. I had not gone far when I exited to his motel. He checked in and I drove around back to his room. I had Brad's convertible and Devon just reached over and pulled out his clothes bag. While he opened the room and went in, I got his dolly and flight case out of the trunk and took it in and closed the door behind me. I wanted to talk some more and he agreed that it would be nice. I launched into my best marriage counseling advice and we had a nice conversation. In the conversation he began to slip in compliments--if he hadn't, I would have been offended--he had already thoroughly checked me out in the car as the wind blew my short skirt and loose deep-cut v blouse. I admit growing up where I did, I'd always heard stories about how savage and well equipped black men were, and here I was sitting on the edge of the bed with one, who was a know womanizer with a penchant for white woman, according to my husband."

Eric, womanizer or not, I admit I unintentionally made the first move. We had talked about 30 minutes and he had his full flight uniform on except the cap. I told Devon I wanted to talk to him some more, but he should really change out of his uniform--my husband always did before he'd let me get down to business. He got up and went in the dressing area of the room where I could not see and changed--I thought--Devon walked out fully nude and sporting a mighty compliment for me. He was beautifully muscled--all over! He asked me if I liked what I saw.

I simply said, "Yes." "I grew up in Alabama, but I've never seen a black man naked."

It was terribly corny, but he said, "I grew up in Houston, but I've never seen YOU naked--don't you think we should even the score!"

He walked over to me and without asking he started to unbutton my blouse. I didn't stop him--it was so forbidden from every thing in my childhood upbringing it made this encounter more exciting than anything I'd ever done, except the sexual dance I'd been doing with you, Eric. I touched him and he touched me and before I knew it, we were in a wild but short make out party on the bed. He was not a gentle man and I liked it. He rolled me over on my back, spread my legs and I took him and placed him into my wet vagina. As I encircled his black back with my long white legs, he thrust into me and with his length unseated my diaphragm, and practically pressed against my cervix, pulsed ten

long streams of black sperm into me. I
wanted up, but he held me there--there
was only a small loss of erection--then
he grew hard and took several very long
hard strokes and came in me again just as
strongly as before. He pulled out and
asked if I didn't think the second time
was always better. I am extremely
vaginally orgasmic and with the
excitement of the forbidden nature of
what I had just done, I had chains of
orgasms each time. Now, he was through
with me!

I knew I was in trouble, for there
wasn't enough spermicidal jelly in my
vagina and on my cervix to kill every
thing this black stud had pumped into me.
I got dressed as quickly as possible as
he pretended I didn't even exist, and I
ran out to my car. I sat down in the
car's leather bucket seat and I realized
I didn't have my panties--the Bastard had
taken them for a souvenir! I could feel
back flow from my well dilated vagina--
that was good--get him out of me. My
husband kept his golf clubs in the trunk,
and I got his towel--better a golf towel
washed, than pale yellow stains on his
white leather seat. I drove toward the
Woodlands and swore to call his wife, but
I never did. I noted the time as I came
near the Village Center and there was
what I needed--a white company car--Eric
you were in the grocery store.

On the way into The Woodlands, I
thought of what I would do if I were
pregnant with a black man's baby--I
couldn't abort, because I didn't believe
in murdering a child--if I had a black
man's baby all of my family would disown

me, and my husband would put two and two
together and divorce me, tear my girls
away from me...The scary thing was I
might be impregnated as I drove--today
was my most fertile day--the day Brad and
I were going to make a baby boy for him."

Suppose, I still had time I thought,
what could I do--what might stop it or
minimize the probabilities--then I
remembered I'd read about studies that
showed that women who had multiple
partners at the same time rarely get
pregnant, but if they do, it is from the
superior sperm that wins out--they had
said the men's sperm, war with each other
to fertilize the egg. I knew of several
men I'd been with recently, who would
gladly accept the task--but the Warrior I
would be honored to give me a baby was I
believed, far superior to the black man
who had just come in me. I hurried to
the Village Square and found you. I led
you to your car, and we got in. I told
you little, but asked you to drive behind
Randall's in the sloped loading dock
where we could not be seen. I asked you
to come to the passenger's side, I got
out, and you got in dropped the seat back
flat, unzipped your suit pants and pulled
them and your briefs down--there was my
Warrior and I climbed on top of you,
closed the door and guided you into me
and begin to ride as I explained in
detail. You wanted summary--how many
times and how much? You wanted to be sure
you did enough--you ejaculated in me five
times in the hour and each time was far
more than he had.

Ann, after the fifth you collapsed
onto my chest. I told you I did think you

would most likely have a baby from this
day and the baby would be mine. Now you
have to face the fact the baby is mine
not your husband's. Your baby will most
likely be a boy--I make them about 85% of
the time. You've seen my three sons--two
of them are much alike, the middle one is
not you're probably going to get a match
to me or one of the two who look alike.
Are you OK with that? If this isn't
enough, you may want to seek others right
away.

Eric, I was more than OK, and I sought
no others and Bradley is yours without a
doubt. I still wanted what you had talked
of as 'The Forest' and after our baby
arrived and the recovery period was up, I
came to you again. You were my first (not
even my husband), after the arrival of
the baby and I showered on you attention
in every way to make you know how much I
valued my Warrior. At the end of the four
hours I could spend with you, you said
you still wanted to cherish me.

Ann I had my spies out, your husband
was gone for several days, his mother was
in for a visit and wanted you to go away
so she could have the children to
herself, Desiree and the boys went to
grandparents for a week, and I took two
days off--so I had a messenger bring a
letter to your door announcing you had
won a 48 hour stay at a famous hotel and
spa near the Galleria and that a limo
would pick you up in two hours. At the
bottom was the instruction to call a
number and use the code word "Warrior" if
you would be ready. You did, it did and I
was in it and we did go to be best hotel
in the Galleria and spent two glorious

days together. You learned about 'The Hunter' and 'Sex, Honor, and Love, without Constraints' and you never again used the word Warrior in referring to me. I cherished you properly, so I will always remember you.

Eric, 'My Hunter,' I slipped up sometime on those two days or you dislodged my protection this time and I didn't notice--with men like you running around--thank god for birth control pills anyway, Bradley has a brother named Brent and he is yours. You moved away I would have told you. My husband, Brad loves his three daughters, but we might as well say it--he loves his two boys more, and doesn't have a clue he had some help in getting them.

*Desire Davidson*

# Ripe Fruit

Jennie worked for "M" and I had just bought over ten million dollars of communication equipment from her. It made her sales goal for the next two years and she was very grateful. Jennie was fat, but she knew how to dress and if you closed your eyes and listened to her voice, you heard a beautiful woman, and her personality was wonderful. If only she wasn't fat I'd thought many times before, when she called on me at HPL.

Jeannie came to see me after the huge purchase was received by the "M" business office and accepted. She wanted to thank me by taking me to lunch in the best restaurant in downtown Houston, located in the best hotel in town. It was a wonderful lunch and Jeannie wanted to talk afterward. I called my Secretary and told her not to expect me back, since I was still at lunch and it was two o'clock in the afternoon. Jeannie had paid the check long before and we continued to sit there having coffee, cheesecake with raspberries and sauce whipped cream and talking.

She took an envelope from her briefcase and laid it on the table in front of her. Then, she said, "I want you to look at this information before you leave, but I have to leave now for a sales meeting at the office."

I stood up and shook her hand and as she walked away I thought how beautiful she could be if she just had help in losing those extra pounds--maybe she would.

I sat back down and drank my coffee. Here I was 34 years old, 6' 2," 180 pounds and I wondered if I would ever get fat as I aged. I was just about to get up to go when I noticed the envelope lying partially under Jeannie's napkin.

I sat back down and reached for the envelope. I opened it and there was a note and a smaller envelope. The note said Jeannie wanted to show her appreciation for the sale and she knew I liked 'finer things.'

"Have a little gold for your gold, enjoy!" she wrote.

I opened the smaller envelope; inside were a door card key for the hotel and a note giving the corresponding room number. I was curious.

I finished my coffee and headed to the elevators to the large suite level. I thought since I was going to a huge suite, that I would find Jeannie and her associates throwing me a surprise party for making their division the highest grossing division in company history. I opened the door and in the setting room there were so many flowers it looked like a funeral. There were also several trays of ripe fruits, appetizers and drinks. I stood there for a moment and there was not a sound. Then I saw a trail of rose petals leading into the next room. They led to a smaller sitting room, the door leading out had rose petals leading to the door and disappearing under it.

There was a note taped to the door. Jeannie's handwriting said "Have a wonderful time--I hope this is your

passion." I opened the door and there was
a drop-dead gorgeous young woman standing
by the bed in very haut couture clothing.

I said, "Hi, I'm Eric what's your
name?"

She replied, "Roxanne."

I closed the door behind me and took a
few steps and stood right in front of
her. I took her hand and said, "So you're
my present?"

She said, "That's what they tell me--
anything you want."

I told her I would like to get out of
my suit, but for her not to do anything
because I wanted to undress her. I peeled
off my clothing in record time and
approached her with a fully naked body
with my cock fully erect and bobbing with
each heart beat.

"My God, you're big!" She said.

"I said I hope we will both have
special memories of this time.

I said, "May I have the privilege now
of undressing you?"

"You may," she said.

I removed the slim double strand gold
belt from her waist and laid it aside.
The sheer black cashmere sweater had to
come over her head, but did very little
to mess up her beautiful long blond hair
spiraled in the latest style.

As I took her sweater off, I said,
"You are a gorgeous golden surprise!"

She had on a sheer maroon bra and its
C-cups were filled with sweet firm ivory
breasts. I undid the front close clasp
and took the bra away from her body. I
asked Roxanne to sit on the edge of the
bed and I took her small feet and removed
the cutest high heels. They were black

patent leather and had a strap up each
side meeting at her ankle and then
connected to a loop around the ankle with
a tiny gold clasp. After I laid them
aside I noticed her stockings. She was
wearing a very sheer smoky grey mist
stocking. These were real stockings and
not panty hose. I asked her to stand up
and I unzipped her, just-below-the-knee,
tweed skirt. The skirt was an interwoven
fabric with black, grey and maroon little
dots making up its primary color of smoky
maroon. The skirt had a conservative slit
at the side and could have been worn by
any secretary except from its feel, the
skirt was cashmere. I lowered her skirt
to the floor and she stepped out of it.

Now my gorgeous golden surprise was
standing in front of me. I purposely did
not touch her bare body as I was
unwrapping the package one part at a time
and then I could play with my new toy
later. I asked her to sit again, and I
removed the stockings as I unclipped them
from the maroon garter belt, I then had
her stand and I removed it. The panties
were left. They were very sheer maroon
with little gold ribbons at each side. I
took the bows of the French cut panties
and pulled them releasing her last
delicate covering. I placed them with the
other clothing and then came to her.

I took my little blond doll in my arms
and bent to her and kissed her
passionately. She returned the kiss just
as passionately. As we continued to kiss,
my free hand explored her wonderful
breasts and then moved to explore her
golden crowned pussy. She was well

lubricated and was ready for anything I
wanted to do.

We continued to kiss and then I
stopped. I picked Roxanne up in my arms
and moved around the big California king
size bed, and laid her on the bed far
enough for me to lie down as well. She
moved on her side and in our common
positions I was looking into her
beautiful blue eyes. I told her she was
the most gorgeous woman I'd been with in
many years. I pulled her to me and began
to kiss her again as my hard cock was
tracing a thick line of pre-cum across
her firm flat tummy.

As we kissed I fondled her big erect
nipples and her lovely breasts. The ivory
of her breasts was the color of her
entire body. She had guarded herself very
well from the sun. I was trying to gauge
how old she was and I think she must have
read my mind for she told me 'my gift'
was 26 years old. We began to talk a bit.
She reached down and took my big thick
cock in her hand and marveled at its
size.

"Don't you ever get soft?" she asked,
"You've been hard since you came in the
door."

I told her she was keeping me that way
and there would be a use for it later.
"I'll be sure and make my pretty baby
come," I said.

"Oh, I don't come," she said. "Oh, I
fake it for my clients but I can't come
without a vibrator."

I asked her if I could place my
fingers in her. I reached down to her
golden crowned pussy and opened her lips
and looked at her clit. It was not large,

but it was prominently positioned. I
placed my index finger in her and felt
for her G-spot. It was well engorged. I
placed two fingers in her against
significant tightness. I needed her
relaxed to three fingers to easily take
my thick cock.

"Do you come from oral sex—
cunnilingus?" I asked. Her reply was no.

I moved back up and positioned myself
face to face with her. I said, "I would
like to make you come with my tongue and
I want you to be honest with me that you
will not fake orgasms. I lay down on my
back with a pillow folded and placed it
under my head to give the correct angle,
and then I asked her to straddle my face.
I opened her pussy lips and began to give
her the nicest licks and flicks of all
with my tongue. As I did this I reached
up and fondled her gorgeous breasts.
After about ten minutes her legs began to
quiver and tighten against my head and
the pretty little baby was crying out in
pleasure as wave after wave of orgasms
rocked her body.

She moved off of me and smothered my
mouth with kisses.

All the while she exclaimed, "I never
felt like that! I never felt like that!"

We repositioned face to face lying on
our sides.

"See, you can come with my tongue," I
said.

I reached down to her pussy and slid
in one, two and then three fingers into
her. The orgasms had relaxed her and she
was prepared to receive my oversized
cock. I went back to kissing her and then
told her I would like to fuck her now. I

want it to be face to face. Normally since you are so little I would do 'woman astride,' 'from behind on hands and knees' or in a 'spoon' position. But I want to see your face when you come. I want to look into your eyes as we are making love. She seemed very small as I loomed over her, and moved between her marvelous legs. My cock was dripping clear pre-cum liquid as I positioned over her body and the clear drops were gathering in a small pool just above her silky blonde pussy hair. I asked her to take my cock and place it in her vagina. I had been wanting this hot little girl so long I was almost afraid I'd come too soon for her to achieve her pleasure.

The head of my cock was firmly in her and I slowly and gently opened her little pussy. I 'bottomed out' at about 9 inches. I made a mental note to not go for full penetration in my ecstasy of taking her for the first time. I stopped and allowed her to completely adjust to my size, and then I began long slow motions in and out of her. As she relaxed further, I began rapid hard thrusts. I alternated up angle thrusts with down angle thrusts to stimulate the G-spot as well as the clit. In about 10 minutes my pretty little baby was coming on me.

After she had come for about 5 minutes, I was at my limit with her tight friction stimulating me wonderfully. I began to shoot stream after stream of creamy white cum into her beautiful body. It felt so good to make love with her and fill her with my cum! As we finished, I moved off of Roxanne and lay down beside her. I returned to kissing her again and touching her breasts.

When the afterglow had subsided, I moved on to my back, folded a pillow under my head, and pulled my golden baby onto my face.

I repeated the earlier treatment and enjoyed watching her nipples respond to her coming. It very rarely happens, my cock became again fully erect and was angled just right to be pointing up at her lower back and buttocks and I was so excited in having her to play with, that I began to shoot cum onto her without any physical stimulation. I came with her.

When she dismounted I took her to the huge shower and we spent a long time soaping each other's bodies. My black body hair clung in channels as I rinsed the soap from me. My precious lover's skin glowed under the jets of hot water. She took my cock and washed it as if she were caring for a royal scepter. We decided to make love in the shower. I took her from behind and I cradled her wet glorious breasts as she began to come. I continued to piston into her until I could resist no longer. I shot stream after stream of come into her delicious body...

For the first time I thought to ask her how long her assignment was to last. She told me eight hours.

We continued to play up to the last 30 minutes. I was lying on the bed with a full erection. She went out to the fruit tray and returned with a half of a very ripe peach and she squeezed the juice out over the head of my cock. Then she went down on me and with mouth stretched to

the limit, brought me to orgasm and
joined my cream with the ripe fruit
juice.

We showered together and I dried her
glorious body and then I asked her if I
could have the privilege of dressing her.
I wished I could have kept the pretty toy
and I was symbolically putting her back
in the wrapping paper of her beautiful
soft garments. She was the best thank you
gift I had ever received.

*Desire Davidson*

# A London Delight

Chelsea was the most beautiful of the women I picked up on my trip to London and on to the ancient city of Cairo, Egypt. I saw her walk out of a doorway leading to second floor apartments. She had on black high heels which could be seen as her cute bell bottom jeans swished about her feet. Topping the jeans, she had a white camisole topped by a long red "U" neck sweater with long sleeves coming down onto her hands. She had beautiful long blond hair rolled in long relaxed spirals.

It was crowded at 8 pm in the Piccadilly district of London, and because she was short and thin, I lost her in the crowds. My loss I thought, I would have loved to have met her and killed her softly with kisses and orgasms.

I looked around for about half an hour and I couldn't get the pretty little bell-bottomed clad girl out of my mind.

I decided to have something to eat in a small eatery advertising a special on fish and chips. I went in and placed an order for the 'special' and a Coke. I was looking for a place to sit in the crowded little hole in the wall, when I saw her sitting alone at a table. I walked up to her and asked if I could sit with her. She nodded yes, and I sat down and introduced myself as Eric.

She replied, "I'm Chelsea."

"Are you an American?" she asked, as I looked deeply into her green eyes.

She said, "Tell me about America."

I said, "America is a vast country of 300 million people and over 150 million of them are women, and only a few of them are as beautiful as you, Chelsea!"

She had a classically beautiful face and full lips. They were covered in a bright shade of red matching her sweater. We ate our fish and chips and came to know a few things about each other. She told me she was 31 and a bookkeeper and lived just up the street. I told her I was 46 and an electrical engineer and I'm on my way to Cairo, Egypt for a business meeting.

She said, "Other than a trip across the channel to Paris I have never traveled."

I told her she was lucky to be at home.

"I was not lucky;" I said, "I have traveled to 20 countries and the District of Columbia and 37 states of the 50 United States in my work."

She said, "I wish I could stay and hear about your travels but I have to call my 'Mum.' I told her I would check in at 9:00 pm and let her know how my new job is going."

Then Chelsea said, "Come with me to my flat and after my call, you can tell me all about your travels."

I went with her. In the US we would call her flat a studio apartment with everything together except the bathroom.

She placed her call at 9 pm. It was interesting to hear her crisp British accent. While she talked, I looked at a magazine and then picked up a book off the floor--a book about modern philosophy. In about 15 minutes, she 'rang off' and came and sat on the arm of the big chair where I was sitting. She looked over my shoulder at what I was reading. I put the book down on the floor where I had found it.

Just to see what she would do, I pulled her off the arm and into my lap and kissed her. She kissed back--always a good sign.

Chelsea was a little girl and fit nicely in my lap. I am 6'2" and of medium build and her weight at about 105 pounds was nothing.

My cock was hard and I'm sure she could feel it against her bottom for she said, "My, you are a ready one!"

I said, "I will always be ready for you." I'm thinking about carrying you over to that bed and getting better acquainted.

Chelsea said, "Let's get better acquainted."

She passionately kissed me again with her full red lips. I stood up taking her with me in my arms, and carried her a few feet to the bed. I lay her down with her feet sticking over the edge of the bed and I removed her cute black patent high heels. I unbuttoned her bell bottom jeans and pulled then from her great looking legs. I sat her up and took her long bright red sweater off and laid it on the chair where I had placed her jeans. I then took her camisole and panties off and I had a beautiful naked lover ready to play.

While I took my clothes off, Chelsea turned down the bed and showed me her beautiful firm ass. She got into bed and I joined her. She turned her back to me and we spooned allowing me full access to her lovely, firm breasts. My cock pressed through her legs and was against her naked blond pussy. I held her and kissed her neck and her beautiful hair. My hands roamed over her firm B-cup breasts and played with her large pink nipples. I told her I wanted to make love to her and she moved onto her back.

I moved on top of her and she took my cock and placed me in her wet pussy lips and I gently eased into her. She was small and tight on my big cock and it felt wonderful. I fucked her with long slow strokes until the pretty baby began to come, each orgasm stronger than the last. We fucked for about 15 minutes and then both of us exploded in climax. I flooded her little body with my creamy white cum and she just kept on coming as I continued to move in her. I was not a young man anymore, but her visual picture was so stimulating beneath me I could stay hard for her to finish. I pulled out of her still mostly hard and she went down on me and left pretty red lipstick marks on my cock as she sucked me totally hard again. She knew how to treat a man's cock. Soon, she had me coming in her mouth and she couldn't take it all, so I shot cum all over her beautiful breasts and then I kissed and licked her breasts.

Chelsea stroked my cock back hard again and she mounted woman astride. The naughty, little, bitch rode me like a rodeo rider on a bucking bronco and again

I flooded her pussy with cum. She collapsed in joy onto my hairy chest and her golden blond hair covered me. I asked her if she now had enough of the 'United States?'

She replied, I'm just starting the 'British invasion,' and indeed she engaged me in love making all night long. Starting with a sensuous bath for both of us and long loving sessions through the night, we became one. Our finale was a soft delicious session face to face so I could look into her pretty green eyes as we came with each other.

I woke holding her and I had to rush to the 'tube' (subway) to get back to my hotel and then on to my flight to Cairo out of Heathrow.

*Desire Davidson*

# A Closer Encounter

Diane and I quickly undressed each other as we stood in my hotel room.

* * *

After all the passengers were all loaded, our aircraft had been disabled when a fuel transfer pump failed in the pilot's check list of critical items. They kept us on the plane for two hours because Portland, Oregon maintenance thought they might be able to fix the problem without replacing the pump. They were wrong and the flight was cancelled.

I was in first class on my way to Seoul, South Korea. Diane was our flight attendant and a great flirt and was quickly moving to the head of my list of people I wished I could be with tonight. Diane was like a sparkling diamond set aflame by pure white light. She had a great personality, intelligence, a powerful sexiness and great looks. I estimated she was in her late twenties. From her banter she knew what she wanted, and if at all possible, I was going to give it to her.

* * *

Diane and I pulled down the bed coverings of the king size bed.

* * *

I had lucked out and was staying at the same hotel as the flight crew and having registered in front of her, I handed Diane my business card. I had written my room number on the back of the card and the words "You are beautiful-- I'd love to show you just how much, Eric."

- 101 -

\* \* \*

I had been in my room only a few minutes when I heard a soft knock on my door. It was Diane. As she came in she handed me my card and said she wanted to cash it in. I took it from her and took her in my arms and kissed her very passionately. After breaking the embrace, we began to undress. The sexual tension was so strong that we jumped onto the bed and we started making out like two teenagers.

My cock slipped into her easily--she was very excited from our flirtation on the plane. When fully in her, I told her how good she felt! I bent down and sucked her nipples--they were about the size of my little finger tip and about a third of an inch when fully erect. She had B-Cup breasts and they were beautiful.

As her pussy adjusted, I began to move in a continually more rapid pace. Diane began to come and I helped her on for about ten minutes and then I began to shoot stream after stream of cum into her great little cunt.

When I finished, I moved out of her and saw her neatly trimmed dark red bush dripping with my creamy seed. I held her in my arms and kissed her pretty little freckles. Her shoulder length dark red hair cascaded over the bed pillow. She was a beautiful little sex partner.

Diane was very orgasmic, and I loved to see a woman enjoy sex like she did. We lay and kissed and fondled and in about 15 minutes she was ready to play again. I asked her to take me in the 'woman astride' position. She moved over me and eased down on my long, thick cock. She had a great pussy for extended play; she lubricated easily and remained tight even under significant stretching required to accept me. In short she was fantastic. She rode me like a Wyoming cow girl riding a bucking horse and the intensity of her cries reflected her intense orgasms. She would take me to the edge of coming and I would resist and let her go on her orgasmic way. Finally, I could resist no more and I blasted my seed into her lovely cunt.

Diane collapsed on my hairy chest and fell asleep. I was still hard and I remained in her until she woke in about an hour and had another ride.

I was in one of my manic moods again, I didn't need sleep and I was driven to have sex. We played several more hours interspersed with soft touches and passionate kisses. Finally Diane said she had to sleep to be ready for the 16 hour flight tomorrow. I held her as she slept and gently kissed her forehead at her hairline as I stirred her awake at 6 am. She joined me in the shower and we had a fun soapy time followed by the intense stimulation of drying each other. We got dressed and she joined her crew to prepare the plane to receive passengers. We had been in the air about 4 hours when she came and sat in the empty seat next to mine.

Diane whispered in my air, "Are you a member of the mile high club?"

"No," I said.

"Do you want to be?" she said. "If you do, get up and go to the First Class restroom and prepare yourself and I'll be in the galley for a few minutes and then I'll come in and join you," she said.

I did as instructed. Diane came into the rest room. As I sat, my cock was standing at attention in anticipation. Diane pulled her skirt up and her panties aside and settled on my cock. She felt great. I asked her if she had ever had an orgasm this way. She told me no. I replied that things were about to change. She rode me with her back to me and the head of my cock massaged her 'G-spot' until she was coming violently. She was biting her hand to keep from crying out. When I felt she had experienced enough, I shot stream after stream of cum into her fantastic pussy. Diane put herself together and left and spent some time in the galley. I put myself together and I returned to my seat. In a few minutes Diane came and sat in the empty seat beside me. We were softly laughing about the experience. It had been unbelievably hot for both of us.

Diane said, "I think we joined wonderful clubs today--you the mile high and me coming on a big cock for the first time in the air."

Just before we arrived she said, "I have a two day layover in Seoul and I'd love to spend more time with you, Eric."

I said, "I staying at the Renaissance Hotel, and I would welcome your pretty, naked, little body in my bed anytime."

We had a wonderful time those two days and I suppose she left me a gift. When I was getting clothes out of my suitcase a few days later I found in the bottom Delta Gold Wings stamped 'Diane.'

*Desire Davidson*

# Out of the Shower

I had never been anywhere in South America and my Spanish was rotten, but here I was sitting in Quito, Ecuador. I'd be here for a month to manage the native engineers in designing an electrical variable speed driver pump station to be added to the Trans-Andean Pipeline.

The native engineering manager and I did not hit it off immediately, but when I brought him a painting after visiting a 'crafts' fair, every thing was cool. I had noted his computer's screen saver was a pretty naked senorita lying back on a huge motorcycle; I knew what he would want.

I couldn't give him a motorcycle or the senorita, but I brought him a painting of a beautiful senorita lying on a backdrop, wearing a festival mask so the upper portion of her face was covered and all she had on were knee high, green socks. I handed the package to him and on tearing open the paper, he was so excited he was immediately looking for a hammer to hang the painting on his wall.

I was watching him hang it when Mercedes, the 23 year old Office Manager, handed me several papers to sign. She was very close showing me where to sign

She said quietly, "The painting is nice, but I'd look better in that costume."

I stood up as she did and I handed the papers back to her and our hands accidentally touched.

I looked directly into her dark green eyes and said "I would very much like to see her in that pose."

Mercedes was a doll. She was about 5'3" and had naturally curly black hair that she wore down around her shoulders. She was of slim build, but she had large 'D-Cup' breasts. She was wearing a thin cotton dress blouse and a short yellow skirt that accented every curve... She was a living doll.

A few days later my driver was sick and Mercedes came to pick me up at my hotel in the morning. As she drove away I noted she had on dark green knee high socks.

"Was it possible?" I thought.

The day went quickly and Mercedes came to my office to see if I was ready to go. I told her I would be just a minute, to sit down. She had on a short skirt about nine inches above the knee and the skirt was a plaid and its short length highlighted her green stockings. She was wearing a matching plaid vest over a white eyelet blouse. She really looked great! Soon, I was logged off and locked up and ready to go. We went to the parking garage and climbed into her vehicle and she headed out to my Hotel.

"Mercedes," I said, "Will you join me for dinner?"

Mercedes agreed and went up to my room so I could take a quick shower. I was certain I was going to have this little South American doll, but I didn't know how--I couldn't read her face or eyes--I didn't have to.

Mercedes came up to my room to see if the company was getting the room the hotel was charging her for. She asked to use the bathroom. Then when she came out I went in and took my shower. As I dried myself I was oozing pre-cum. Mercedes asked me to come out and I wrapped a towel around my waist. When I came out Mercedes was on my bed and was in the pose of the painting I had given Carlos. She was beautifully naked except for her green stockings and the festival mask covering her eyes and nose.

Mercedes said, "What do you think, Eric, am I better than the painting?"

I said, "You're much better; you are beautiful and fully alive!"

Mercedes told me to take my towel off and sit down on the couch. I did and she came to me and knelt in front of me. Her breasts were beautiful and begging to be touched.

Mercedes touched my fully erect cock and said, "I see the other girls in our office building have not been lying.

"Am I too late to get the best treatment?" she asked.

"You are not too late--you are just in time--please help yourself," I said.

Mercedes took my cock in her delicate hand and began to tongue its head. She still had on the mask and it made it even more exciting to have her licking and sucking me incognito. She mastered taking me and in a few minutes she had me coming in her mouth. She rose up to me and with her hard nipples thrust into my chest, she French kissed me and gave me back my cum. She then led me by the hand to the king sized bed. We lay down and kissed for awhile and I asked to take her mask off.

She said, "It is not permitted."

I moved between her legs and found her firm clit with my tongue and very quickly brought her to long strings of orgasm. When I moved away she reached down and pulled me up on top of her. The sexy masked girl was a little tight for entry for my over sized cock, but shortly she opened like a flower and I penetrated her fully. We fucked for fifteen minutes and she was coming practically all the time. Then I came and filled her tight little pussy with my semen.

She said, "Oh damn, my diaphragm slipped off when you were thrusting so deep.

I said, "Don't worry I'm a safe play toy, I had a vasectomy thirteen years ago.

She seemed relieved. We sixty-nined and then fucked again. She was wonderful. She got up from the bed and went to the rest room and when she returned, she still had her mask on. She dressed with it on and I dressed as well.

When she was fully dressed, she kissed me and asked me to take the mask off. I did and as it cleared her face she said, "Senor Eric I will ask the hotel to make some adjustments for your comfort."

It was a very clear signal that all between us was private and without the mask she was the Office Manager. I kept the mask and had the pretty little girl over six times before I headed back to the United States. She was more playful each time and was my best memory of Quito, Ecuador.

# Can You Read My Mind

"Can you read my mind?" I thought, as I sat down on a couch in the hotel lobby. Only a table separated us and we were both doing the same thing--looking at the Philadelphia visitors' guide.

She was truly a beautiful woman. She had deep auburn hair framing her classically beautiful face. Even as far away as I was, I could look over my book and catch glimpses of bright emerald eyes. She had just the right number of freckles on her legs and I would love to apply an angel kiss to each one. She wore a dark green silk dress that would hit just above the knee if she were standing; as it was it gave a generous view of her beautiful legs. I was most intrigued by the dress for it had buttons all the way down the front. I have always loved real buttons down the front--they invite me to explore. Her lovely neck was accented by a three strand gold necklace. I know real gold when I see it.

I found a place to eat in the restaurant guide section and I put my book down.

Then I said, "Hi, have you found a good place to eat near by."

She looked up and smiled and said, "I just found one."

Coincidentally it was the Italian place about six blocks away that I had found.

I said, "I'm Eric, what's your Name?"

She said, "Caroline."

Caroline, "You have a beautiful name--one I had considered for my daughter but my wife and I never had a daughter--just three sons."

I told her I was an engineer and I had come to Philly for a seminar. In fact it was at 10 Penn Center just across the street from our hotel.

Caroline said, "I'm an Abram's Drug Company rep and I am also in town for a seminar. I travel a lot but call Cleveland, Ohio home."

"Caroline," I said, "Let me take you to dinner at 'Soto Varalli.' We can walk, its only 7 blocks away. It's supposed to be a lovely evening; or we can take a cab."

"Let's walk," she said, "We can see the old city hall that way, and a few other sights."

We got up and left the hotel lobby. The evening air was wonderful for July--it was cool. It was early evening and in about three blocks we did pass Old City Hall. We had walked that distance not holding hands, but now I reached for her hand and Caroline reached for mine and we continued our walk to the restaurant hand-in-hand like two young people.

"Caroline, I said I'm 51"

"I'm 41 she said."

We made it to the restaurant and were in luck, for immediate seating was available for couples. There was a significant wait for larger parties.

Caroline and I were shown to a cozy table in a more dimly lit corner of the restaurant. The waiter asked if we wanted to order a bottle of wine before dinner. Caroline declined. Since I never drink, this girl was my kind of lady. We ordered and then had a wonderful meal of veal parmesan and followed it with strawberry gelato and espresso. The waiter came and I paid the check. The gelato was gone and dishes taken away and we continued to talk.

Caroline had her left hand lying on the table and I reached across with my left and took it in mine. Caroline's right hand was bare of rings which mine was not--I wear a simple gold wedding band, but on her left was a rather exotic ring of several emeralds exactly the color of her eyes. I asked about it. She said it was given to her by a girlfriend.

"What about your gold ring with the heart and shield on it?" she asked."

I said, "It indicates membership in an ages old, secret society. I went on and said that its US temple is here in Philly and I was there last evening, and as a Temple Knight Grand Master Hunter, I was asked to preside over the service with a Grand Master Hunter and a Grand Mistress Huntress of the current course, so all three thrones were filled with me in the middle; 'The Master's Throne.'"

Caroline was interested in the words 'hunter' and 'huntress' and asked about the meaning of the words. And I gave her a brief definition of each.

"What do you do?" she said.

I replied, "I hunt little girls like you and make passionate love to them."

"Like me, or me," she flirtatiously said.

I said, "It could be others or it could be you; it all depends on your decision."

I held both of her hands across the table and for several minutes we stayed that way. I told her she was a doll for coming to dinner with me because I hated to eat alone--much less not have any beautiful hands to hold. She thanked me for the compliment and for the dinner.

As we walked from the restaurant, I felt her hand searching for mine, and holding hands we set out on our seven block walk back to our hotel. At city hall we stopped for a minute and I pulled Caroline to me and I kissed her and she kissed back. We continued kissing from 'friendly' to 'passionate' in the next five or six minutes and then we continued our walk.

I told her how beautiful she was and how much fun I'd had with her this evening.

We arrived at the hotel and entered the elevator and she pushed her floor button which was three floors below mine.

When I pushed the elevator button for my floor, Caroline said, "Oh, get off with me--I have a suite and we can talk some more and besides I want to give you my card for when your in Cleveland."

I followed her to her suite and she got us some cold drinks from the mini bar. We sat and talked. I told her about my grown boys--now men and I told her about my beautiful wife who had to do without me because I was always someplace in the world other than Tulsa, Oklahoma, where we had settled after moving most of our married life.

Do you get lonely 'being on the road' so much?" she said.

"I'm always lonely and longing to be with someone," I said.

"It was wonderful of you to go to dinner with me," I said.

Caroline said, "It is lonely for me too. I have had some very bad relationships with men and I've switched camps almost."

I'd heard this story before.

"I still like the right man, but they are so few and far between. You, I like!" she said.

We were setting side by side on the sofa and I leaned over and gently raised her head in my hand and looking directly into her beautiful green eyes I asked her what she liked about me.

Caroline replied, "I like that you make no demands--you expect me to be totally in control of my fate, and you in yours."

I kissed her gently and said, "Well said."

Then I rose to go.

"No, don't go," she said, "Please stay! I have made my decision. Please let's relieve some of our loneliness and longing--stay with me."

I sat back down. She was almost a little girl the way she asked, but she was a beautiful grown woman.

"Do you want to make love with me?" I asked.

"Yes, I want you--I have decided," she said.

"I want you too," I said. "I wanted you from the moment I sat down across from you in the lobby. I want you now!"

With that I stood up and stood her to her feet, and then I took her in my arms and kissed her. Then I picked her up and carried her to the king size bed in the next room. I lay her down on the bed and took her cute high heels from her feet. She had no stockings--that was why I had observed her beautiful freckles. I removed my shoes and then lay down beside her. We lay on our sides and talked some more and I cautioned her that I might be another 'bad experience with a man'.

She said, "You will not be, I know it from all you've said tonight. I am sure I want you and I will never have any regrets."

I reached for her and kissed her passionately, and said, "I will not have any regrets either."

I told her of my button fetish and asked if I could un-button her dress. We moved off the bed and standing face to face I very slowly un-buttoned each one of her buttons. She had a sheer tan colored B-cup bra and matching bikini panties. She did not wear a slip. I removed the dress from her arms and carefully laid it on the chair. Then I removed her bra exposing fully her pert breasts crowned with medium sized reddish brown nipples and small brown areolas. I traced freckles from her breasts down across her belly with my kisses to the band of her bikini panties. I then knelt and slowly lowered her panties to the floor and took them from her feet as she stepped out. I started at her ankles and kissed a trail of freckles up one leg to her pretty auburn mound. I stood up and pulled her to me again and kissed her and told her how beautiful she was. I removed my clothes and the two of us stood naked. I took her in my arms and picked her up and returned her to the bed. I was hungering badly for her, but I wanted her to be sure.

"Eric your cock looks marvelous!" Caroline said.

I moved between her legs and found her wet and relaxed.

Caroline took my cock in her hand and guided me as I entered her for the first of several times that night. She was marvelous. The tightness of her pussy combined with her silky wetness had me super excited.

I continued long hard thrusts and shortly Caroline began to come.

Oh! God, I'm coming! Don't stop fucking me!" she cried.

I continued long hard thrusts and pushed her to the peak of joy and then I joined her as I shot stream after stream of come into her pretty little cunt.

"You know how to give a man passion in every respect." I said as I collapsed beside her.

In about 15 minutes we were ready again and when you began to come I thrust my big cock deeply into you and filled you again with my come. I stayed hard and began long thrusts again. In another five minutes, I joined your orgasms and erupted in your pussy filling you with stream after stream of creamy white cum.

When we were finished, I went to the bathroom and got a warm wash cloth to clean your delicate cunt. Then I cared for my self and when we were settled

again, I lay behind her and kissed
freckles for several minutes.

Then both you and I were ready again
to make love. Every time was wonderful
and our loneliness and longing did abate
for a time. We were good for each other.

*Desire Davidson*

# The Importance of Good Networking

My flight had been cancelled and I had to take another flight from Tulsa to Cleveland, Ohio. I was tired but mostly hungry when I checked into my hotel.

When I got to my room I took a quick shower and thought about getting in bed, but I was hungry for food and hungry for sex. I put on a Polo shirt and Dockers and slipped into my loafers. There was a restaurant next door. I would walk over and get something to eat; then if an opportunity for female company didn't mature, I would come back and get in bed for a few hours rest.

The hostess showed me to a booth and when I got settled, I looked over to the booth across the aisle and it was Caroline the Drug Rep I met in Philadelphia and also a beautiful blonde.

I waved and said, "Hello, Caroline."

She looked up from her drink and said, "Eric! What are you doing in town?"

I said, "The usual--a control systems project--working with a vendor;

Introduce me to your friend."

Caroline said, "Eric this is Carol-- we've started living together--and Carol this is the Eric from Philadelphia."

I went over and said hello to Carol and I bent over and kissed Caroline. Caroline's auburn hair flowed over the shoulders of a long brown ribbed sweater. She was wearing dark jeans and she had on the sexiest high heels. They were brown plaid with a brown ribbon lacing the sides and heel and coming together in the front in a bow above a rounded toe. Carol had on a dark blue jogging suit and sneakers. Her blonde hair was in long curls and fell onto the blue of the suit.

Carol invited me to set down by her, and she scooted over to make room for me. Carol was a blonde delight. I could just feel sexiness radiating from her and Caroline as well. My waiter came with my drink and I told him I would be joining the girls, to bring my food over here.

Carol said, "Did everything Caroline told me happened in 'Philly' really happen?"

I said, "I guess that all depends on what she told you!"

Carol went on in a teasing fashion and said, "Caroline says you're hung like a stallion. Are you?"

My cock was snaked down my left pants leg and was as hard as rock from just looking at these two beautiful women. I took Carol's right hand and placed it in my lap.

"You tell me," I said.

She touched me and began to laugh, and said "He is--he really is!"

I said, "I would be happy to demonstrate it with you two beautiful women." Carol and Caroline looked at each other and then both nodded. I asked if they wanted to go to my hotel just next door. We finished our food and that's where we went.

I had a suite just perfect for play time, there was king size bed, a couch and two overstuffed chairs and a Jacuzzi tub that actually was open to the bedroom.

As soon as we walked in the door, the girls began to shed their clothes and I followed their lead. In a matter of a minute or two we were three nude sybarites ready to play. I ran the Jacuzzi tub and set the jets, and when I turned around the two little bitches were in a 69 eating each other's pussies. I then realized the full meaning of what Caroline had said in Philly about her ring, because Carol was wearing an identical emerald ring on her left hand. They were bonded bisexuals.

The tub was ready and I got in and relaxed as I watched my little playmates coming and coming with each other. My cock was so stiff from their antics it stood up out of the water.

Carol and Caroline finished with each other with earth shaking orgasms and then joined me in the tub. They were beautiful in the tub with the bubbling water covering their breasts at times and then exposing them. The two were a perfect pair. Both girls had beautiful firm B-Cup breasts and both came with large nipples. Caroline's were brown and Carol's were pink in keeping with her blondeness.

Caroline had soft auburn hair. She scooted over next to me and laid her head on my black hairy chest and sweetly said, "Carol wants you to take her first--make it hard and fast; then it's my turn."

I got out of the tub and helped Carol out. As I dried her off with a big fluffy towel. I spent particular time on her pussy lips and golden haired mound of Venus. Both girls had their hair neatly trimmed. Carol then dried me and spent a special amount of time drying my cock and balls. I thought I was hard before, but now I was really hard and ready for this attractive little girl. When she finished, I picked her up and carried her to my bed. I placed her on it and joined her and moved between her legs. Carol took my cock and placed it in her ready wet pussy and I pushed in slowly.

Caroline, called out, "Remember Eric, fuck her hard and fast--she needs it."

I did just that and very shortly my pretty blond baby was straining all over as wave after wave of orgasms rocked her body. Her tight little cunt was my cock's end, I began to cum in her pussy and I didn't think I'd ever stop coming in her. Soon both of us were finished and I moved beside her and shared the afterglow of wonderful orgasms.

Carol said, "I want you to lick my clit and make me come again."

I folded a pillow for my head and I had her straddle my face and I began my joyful task. As I stimulated her with my tongue, my two hands were busy fondling her firm little breasts and big nipples.

In a few minutes Carol said, "God, you're good--cock and tongue! I've never come so much with a man. I can't make up my mind which is best your cock or your tongue. I want to ride that cock of yours and see!"

I lay on my back and Carol mounted me in the woman astride position and rammed down on my cock; then she began a wild ride that had her coming and crying at the same time. Suddenly I shot streams of cum into her little body as she had her strongest orgasm. It was so strong that she collapsed on my chest with my cock still in her. She lay there and I picked her face up and gave her a passionate kiss and said we were neglecting Caroline.

Carol and I got back in the Jacuzzi with Caroline and we positioned on each side of her and started intense petting, with Carol and me alternating with deep passionate kisses on her mouth. When she was ready, Carol dried Caroline and herself as I also dried off.

The three of us got on the bed and I was completely hard again. Caroline decided to ride me as Carol had done and Carol wanted to straddle my face again and get her pussy eaten out. A threesome ensued. Caroline felt just as good to my cock as she had in Philly and my little friend, Carol was coming the minute my tongue stroked her clit. The two lovely women were a festival of delights. As I shot my cum into Caroline, Carol was drenching my face in wetness.

The two little sexy bitches finally wore me out and they went back to a 69 girl on girl position and gave me a few minutes to recover and then they were ready to go again. Caroline and Carol spent the night with me and I took them separately and together. When we settled down to sleep I had two 'babes' one on each side lying on my black hairy chest.

In the night one or the other would wake
me playing with my cock when they were
ready to make love again and they mounted
me to take a wild orgasmic ride.

# Birthday Sex with Strangers

It was February and for my birthday on the 13th I usually try to treat myself to a sex party and see how many partners I can have in eight hours.

When I was waiting in the bar for my table, I met a woman named Charlotte. She was an attractive blond and was sporting some very pretty breasts as shown by her low cut blouse. I was 51 years old today and I never got tired of pursuing a new sexual encounter. Charlotte would be number 5121 in my sexual inventory. I invited her to dinner and she was a sparkling companion. We had a good time getting to know each other. It was obvious she was going to give me a birthday surprise on this Tuesday night. After dinner she took me back to her apartment and we had a fun time of sexual entertainment. It lifted my spirits because my work assignment was three weeks long and I did not get to go home on the weekends to my wife, Desiree.

Charlotte invited me to stay the night and she so enjoyed me she invited me to stay with her through Friday night. When I came in on Friday, she said she had a belated birthday surprise for me--we were going to a sex party that night.

I had been to many sex parties, so the expanse of naked flesh was not surprising to me.

I asked Charlotte what she would like to do before we split up for the evening. Charlotte answered by going and getting a man that appealed to her. She wanted to impale her delicious ass on Loren, lay back on his chest and let me take her pussy for a double penetration. That is exactly what she did and the naughty little girl started coming shortly after my first entry.    Charlotte was primed for the rest of the party. I might be 51 years old but I still recover quickly, and very shortly I found myself standing in line to gang bang a babe named Alexis.

Alexis was a fiery red head and when I entered her cum soaked pussy I looked into her green eyes and fucked her hard and fast and added my cum to that of the seven men who fucked her before me while I watched.

I went from Alexis and moved to Hope. She was an attractive blonde haired, green eyed, sexy bitch. She took me woman astride and I played with her small, firm breasts the whole time she rode me. When she would come her stiff nipples would soften and then recover their hardness. She rode for about 15 minutes and my cock exploded in her tight cunt and filled her with my cum.

Next I moved to Cassandra. She was about 36 and had beautiful large breasts. She also took me women astride and again I had her delicious breasts to play with the whole time she rode me. I lasted about twenty minutes before I flooded her

with cum. I was slowing down in recovery
so I switched and found a male friend.

Eric had a muscular build and a seven
inch, medium thickness, cock. He had
sandy brown hair and he told me he was 44
as we discussed him fucking me in the
ass. He entered me and my cock instantly
came erect. He felt good and I
concentrated on his rhythm and felt the
swell of his cock as he began to shoot
his cum in my ass.

I was about to go back to the women
when James asked if he could suck me off.
We lay on our sides and I thrust my cock
into his mouth. He was a handsome man
with black wavy hair and grey eyes. He
had very little hair on his body--unlike
my bear-like, hairy body. When I came in
his mouth I gagged him with my copious
cum but he managed to take it all. James
sucked me hard again and I wanted a
woman.

I saw Connie a slim little girl with
pert B-cup breasts. She was 37 and after
fucking her face to face, I sucked and
licked her pussy and brought her to a
number of oral orgasms to complement the
ones she had while I was fucking her. She
sucked me hard again and I moved over to
her friend Regina.

Regina was a red headed doll with firm
D-cup breasts. She was 33 and had never
had children and her breasts showed it--
they were perfect. I positioned Regina on
her hands and knees and as I fucked her I
reached under and cupped her breasts.
That brought her off like a fire cracker
and her pussy did its best to milk me
dry.

She took the stiffness out of me and I was flaccid for about 30 minutes so I found Rosemarie and Amanda and got them off with my tongue. Both of them sucked my partially flaccid cock and Amanda brought me to full stiffness again. Another man was waiting to be with her, so I moved on to Donna.

Donna was a real red head complete with green eyes and freckles. I kissed all over her body exploring the freckles and then I mounted her and fucked her face to face. She came easily and the greedy, little, bitch just kept coming. After about ten minutes I cut loose and shot stream after stream of cum into her pretty red haired pussy. I talked to her awhile and it turned out it was her birthday too, she was 31 years old. Since I had already given her my best, I offered her long passionate kisses and gave her the best kisses of all and stimulated her clit with my tongue until she could hardly stand the intensity of her orgasms. I might have fucked her again but Loren was waiting to fuck her.

I moved on to Pamela and I was wiped out in the cum and erection departments and I spent a long time just giving her oral sex while I recuperated. I wanted to end the party on an up note. I had recovered while I was with Pamela and I invited Cassandra to straddle my face while Abby sucked me off. The three of us were coming together in no time.

Not counting Charlotte since she came with me, I had sex with 13 new partners I knew nothing about. It was a rush to have un-protected sex with 3 men and 11 women in a space of about 8 hours.

I gathered up Charlotte and we went to her apartment and made love in the shower. It was a wonderful birthday gift!

*Desire Davidson*

# The Green Hills of Earth

Tulsa has many parks and in them I have had many sexual adventures in the 15 years I've lived here. My favorite sexual adventure in Tulsa took place in Woodward Park. The park has green rolling hills and many big oak trees. I sometimes like to go there and just get away from the hustle and bustle of life, and walk the green hills of earth.

It was a Tuesday in late May and the day was warm but not uncomfortable. I had called my wife and told her I had a dinner scheduled with a vendor and I would be home late. This was regular routine in the job I had as a project engineer. In reality I just wanted some peace and at seven o'clock I knew few if any people would be in the park. I was right, when I pulled into the parking lot there was only one other car. I parked and then walked down the hill and then walked down the stairs which took me down to the little brook with the fountain sculptures. I crossed the brook on an arch bridge and walked out in the small meadow where there is a beautiful bronze life-size sculpture of an Indian with out stretched arms sitting on a sleek horse. I walked to the sculpture and petted the horse as if he were alive. I needed this

kind of walk to just let my imagination
clear the stress of work from my mind. I
started back across the brook and started
my climb up the rolling green hills.
Shortly I realized I was headed right for
a cute woman in light blue shorts and a
white blouse and white sandals. I was
practically on top of her when I saw her,
so I changed my direction to take me 10
feet or so to the right of her.

As I approached, she said, "It is a
beautiful bronze, isn't it?"

I agreed and stopped, standing several
feet from her. She had blond hair, pulled
back in a pony tail and she was very
attractive.

She said, "I always pet the horse,
wishing it could come alive and then I
come up here and sit until the dusk takes
away my view and I am left only with
imagination."

I told her I too would sometimes do
that and then come to the very spot she
was on and set down and watch the
sculpture as the dusk descended.

"I didn't expect a beautiful girl to
be here now," I said.

She said, "I'm sorry I'm in you place.
Come and set with me and share."

I did, and I learned her name was Jill
and she was born in Tulsa 34 years ago,
and she hadn't been out of the city very
many times in her life.

I told her I traveled the world and
all over the United States in my work,
and being away from home wasn't what it
was cracked up to be. I told her I was 47
years old and I was getting tired of
seeing the world.

"I miss seeing beautiful Tulsa girls like you." I said.

She laughed. "So you come to the park and pet the bronze horse to have a tie to home," she said.

I said, "That is pretty much true, but of course my wife lives here and she is my ultimate tie to home."

Jill answered, I'm not married and I get lonely and I don't get called beautiful that often Eric, so it's nice to hear your compliments."

As the dusk came, the Indian and horse began to disappear. We continued to talk to each other as we sat in the semi darkness. The parks department hadn't mowed the park recently and the grass was long and cool and green and soft.

Jill asked, "Eric can you take the time to stay a while and watch the stars come out with me?"

"Yes, I feel like I have all the time in the world sitting here with you," I said.

Jill lay back in the grass and I did too. After a few minutes she reached for my hand and I took her hand as the stars began to appear. The stars were beautiful in the clear sky of a late spring evening. Her hand was warm in mine. We continued talking about everything in our lives that was stressing us and also the good things.

In awhile, Jill asked, "Do you believe in soul mates?"

"I do," I said.

Jill asked, "Are you my soul mate?"

I replied, "I would very much like to be."

Jill asked, "Will you kiss me?"

I leaned over her and began to passionately kiss her.

After a few minutes, she said, "Would you like to make love with me?"

I told her it would be an honor to make love with her.

"Where do you want to?" I asked.

She said, "Why not right here on the soft green grass?"

I began to unbutton her blouse and then took off my shirt. Then I removed her shorts and I removed my pants. I then had her sit up and I removed her bra. In the semi darkness I could see that she had lovely breasts crowned with medium size nipples. I lay her back and then I removed her panties and my briefs followed. Now we were totally naked.

I returned to softly kissing her, and I felt Jill's hand reach for my cock. She took it and slowly stroked it. "My God! You're big!" she said. "You're a girl's delight!"

I touched her slit and found her wet and relaxed enough for a careful entry. I asked her if she wanted me to use a condom.

Jill said, "No, I want to feel you and give myself totally to you. I want you to fill me with your sperm and make me yours."

I moved on top of her and positioned between her legs. She took my cock in her soft warm hand and guided me into her. Her legs came up and encircled my back as I began to fuck her. She had a wonderful pussy--very tight but well lubricated.

Jill said, "You are the first man I've had in six months."

I replied, "I am honored and pleased to be chosen to be your first in such a long time."

Her long legs felt wonderful wrapped around my back as she used them to pull me into her body. We fucked for about ten minutes and she began to come--gently at first but building in crescendo into strong passionate orgasms that were moving me to climax. She was deliciously tight as she contracted in orgasm. I lasted only about five more minutes and then began to shoot my cum into her delicious cunt.

As we finished coming, I moved off her and repositioned on my side, she did the same and we faced each other in the now partial darkness for the moon was rising.

"You're beautiful in moon light," I told her.

I would have loved to have stayed there for ever and made love to her, but it could not be. The park patrol would soon be closing the park for curfew. We dressed and we walked to our cars.

She said, "I want to give you my card." She opened her car door and then shortly she brought me her card.

"So you're an independent artist," I said. "What type of art do you do?"

She said, "With you it will be oil based sensual performance art. Call me when you're ready to enjoy a bed of perfumed oils or want to enjoy the green hills of earth again."

I took her in my arms and kissed her passionately for a long time.

Over the next five years we met many times, usually in her studio apartment, but when the weather was right, she took

me to the green hills of earth and put me
in touch with my soul mate.

*Desire Davidson*

# One Summer

I was out shopping for a few hours one day in early summer of '63 and Pamela had the run of the house and I guess it was time for her. I had answered some of her remaining questions the week before. She went down to the drugstore to get a Coke and some air conditioning for it was so very hot all that summer. There you were, a nice guy she knew, and you wanted to know her very well. As she told it to me, you bought her a second coke and after talking for awhile, suggested you walk her home and get to know each other even better. You were 13 and she was 14 and behind a year and had been in school with you in the spring. She invited you in, and the two of you, sitting on the couch, watching nothing on TV, began to pet. She said she started it. She quickly found you knew more than how to kiss and more than how to touch her, or as she said, 'Mama, I had never felt the way Eric was making me feel!' She moved things along, and as you say, you gave her your special invitation, and it was time for her to choose. Looking back, after all these years, we chose well, but there was a time in the fall of that year when we weren't so sure, but our doubts passed the following year. There always has to be a first time for every girl, and she had decided you were definitely hers. She had waited because I had not and she was born when I was 17.

Knowing, she had a couple of hours before I would be home, and having thought carefully about it, she led you down the hall and showed you her room.

She went to the bathroom and when she
came back you had turned her bed down and
you asked her if she was sure she wanted
you. She nodded. She told me that
standing there you touched her and kissed
her, and asked if this was her first
time, and receiving a yes, you told her
that this would be so gentle, so easy,
that she would want to play all
afternoon.

You then undressed her and lay her
down. It was hot even with the window fan
on full, and you cracked the door for a
little circulation. She was concerned
about the four to five inches of open
door, but you reminded her I wouldn't be
home for a couple of hours. As you moved
to her, she said you were very gently
kissing her, fondling her breasts,
sucking and touching her nipples, and
kissing and stroking her body, when you
suggested making her come with the best
kisses of all. We had talked about that
being the way most girls reach orgasm,
and she wanted to try.

She said after that unforgettable
first orgasmic experience, you asked to
explore her with your fingers. She told
me it was nice and when you were
finished, you told her she was very wet
and relaxed and although the fit would
still be snug, it would be pleasant and
if she really wanted too, then she was
ready to make love. You went on and told
her that her hymen was very thin and
small, and even though her first lover
was going to be somewhat large, you would
like to be hers now.

She said it didn't even hurt, and it
felt great as she became a woman when you

gently pushed into her. When you began to move, she said she felt like coming and did, just like when you had kissed and tongued her so sweetly at first. She came, when you made love to her for her very first time! She said after a very long time, she felt your strong long pulses as you finished completing her woman hood. Then you gently pulled out of her, moved from her wrapped legs, and lay beside her. You continued to love her with kisses and words and touches, and she said your hardness felt wonderful, it strongly pushed against her body, and she knew it was insisting you wanted her more.

The one thing she asked me about was that experience. She said from the moment she petted with you on the couch and after having come in her several times, you had never lost your hardness. I told her, "Baby, it just doesn't happen that way with men--you must be mistaken!" She was pretty insistent you had remained that way as the two of you continued delighting in each other, throughout the afternoon.

You taught her some fun positions and interesting things to do. The next to last time, you had her positioned 'woman astride.' You both had lost track of time. As I came in the house and passed the head of the hall, mixed in with the fan noise, I heard what I thought was me vocalizing my orgasms! Then I realized the voice was younger-my Baby! I fought myself. Not wanting to interrupt those sounds, and yet at the same time, I had to at least see that Pamela was alright.

I quietly walked down the hall and through the opening of Pamela's door. I could see the two of you making love. 'This is my Baby's first time?' quickly flashed through my mind. She was coming over and over again as she bounced so very hard up and down on you. I wondered if my daughter had lied to me about being a virgin all the times we had talked about sex, starting when she was 11, and most recently just last week. She certainly didn't look like one, then.

When she finished, your semen dripped out of her as she lay down on your chest. You were pinned beneath her and you had only partially come for you continued, for a considerable time, to seep out between your nestled sides. She'd dismounted too soon, and it was obvious you weren't finished with her yet. As I had this thought, I realized you were looking straight into my eyes and you seemed not to be disturbed I was there watching you. I recalled my previous thought, and I turned and silently walked down the hall and out of the house and let the two of you continue.

My husband wouldn't be home for three hours and I decided to give you two, to continue my daughter's education and for her to reward you by sending you away satisfied. When I came back, you were gone and she was clothed and asleep on her bed. My husband came home and asked where Pamela was. I told him she'd really done too many things today with one of her friends and she was sleeping, and probably was much too tired to wake before morning. The next morning, my husband was off to work, and Pamela came running down the hall to the kitchen calling out that she really needed to talk. Just hearing her recount her first adventure, was almost more than I could stand—not from anger, and not from concern for her, but from vicarious excitement.

She told of a beautiful experience. But I had to remind her we'd talked about the importance of using protection. I reminded her that they were in my nightstand and always available to her without question. Then Pamela told me she obtained them from my room and had tried, but then consciously chose not to use them. She continued to say your bare skin felt so good and she didn't think she could come any other way. For this mother, this wasn't very re-assuring for the future. For, I knew from her description of her first time, you'd be with my daughter any time she wanted you and any time you wanted her. It would be a good while before she tried a second guy as long as you were available. As she had said, 'You were just so much fun! I don't want another guy, he's my first, he's amazing, and I want him for a very long time. I chose the right one!'

As far as I know, I was the only boy she was with that summer. She wanted to make love all the time and she became almost too much to handle as she wanted to explore everything she'd ever heard about and expected you to keep up with her amazing body, and then she had an imagination for new things to try. She found that, yes, you had the stamina for most of her adventures, but you were certainly not 'endless' in anyway.

One day when you were coming out of the drugstore, I was walking down the sidewalk right toward you, and I had an expression of foreboding.

I walked right up to you and said, "We've got to talk! Will you come with me to my house?"

You said, "Sure Mrs.…"

We walked to my car and drove a few blocks to my house.

It was burning hot and I was dressed for it. My pink shorts, white midriff blouse, light pink jewelry, and sexy pink sun glasses made me feel cool, even if it was not. My long black hair shimmered in the sun. You followed me in. You waited for me to settle things in the kitchen and give some direction to this meeting.

I told you to set down at the kitchen table, and when you were seated, I turned around and leaned over the table and took my sun glasses off and you looked into my grey blue eyes, a perfect match for your beautiful long black hair. I could feel your eyes caressing every part of my body. I was a 'hot' mom! And not because the house was stifling, except I did feel a hint of a cool breeze from down the hall. My husband had installed a window air conditioner in the master bedroom. Pamela hold told me that you'd enjoyed the cool with her on three visits. When she first led you to my room instead of hers, you had balked. She explained I had told her she could use my bed with her friend, and reminded her to be on your side by your night stand so she would have no problem remembering to use protection.

You smiled at me as you continued to look at me and when I smiled back, I knew you wanted to possess me. My look softened, and I became friendly. I offered you some ice tea, and we sat at the kitchen table. It seems like only yesterday.

Eric, I was mad. Although it was OK, what you and Pamela were doing, it wasn't OK that you two were not using protection. Pamela was my gift at age 17 for not having protection when I had my first time at age 16! Pamela, told me you were always willing, but she wasn't, because you couldn't penetrate her fully without pulling off, or breaking, or even failing one just getting it on.

"Do you know how to properly use protection?" I asked.

You replied, "Yes, but that's not exactly the problem."

I then took up my daughter's complaint and asked you if it was really because she thought bare feels so much better.

"Well it does." you said. "But we both want to protect her from pregnancy if we can, but oral is not enough for her anymore–she's way beyond that now, having had me for her first, and she has embraced more diverse adventures with every one of the follow on seven sessions since her first."

I then firmly told you that condoms did protect against pregnancy, but they also protected against disease. You told me you knew, but you had never had anything, but you hadn't had much experience, Pamela was your 199th lover. I admit at that moment, all Pamela had told me and that brief 'my own eyes'

experience of seeing the two of you
together the first time, flashed through
my mind. My God! I thought. You are 13
what will your count be in 20 years? Then
I rejected it as fantasy and didn't want
to believe it.

I asked, "If you had said 9th partner?"

You calmly said no. Then almost in a
reverie you said, "I want my 200th soon,
no later than this summer."

I said, "Does anyone know about you?"

At age 13, you told me you never told
anything unless it was life critical-all
of your life was a secret. You told me
you particularly never told anyone about
your encounters. You said only you and
your partner knew who you were and the
details of your private encounters. If
your passion was public, it would be like
the brags of guys saying they had been
with someone when actually they were
virgins themselves.

"I never tell anything!" you said.

I changed the subject, for I was 31
years old and sexually active since age
16 and I had been with 18 men other than
my husband, and I thought I was somewhat
advanced in those very private times of
the 50's and early 60's before birth
control pills changed thinking, even in
the Bible Belt. I was feeling just a
little too curious.

Here, was a boy, loving my daughter,
and he had more experience than almost
all men gain in a lifetime. But I was
burning to know and see what you actually
would tell, and I asked what age range
you had been with. You told me your
oldest was 27 but most were older than
you because you looked older. You said

you loved girls and women of every age, and you felt certain this summer the upper age would change.

I changed the subject again and talked about other things while I decided what to do. I could leave you with my daughter, I could forbid you to see her-- no telling what creep she would then be playing with or I could encourage your safety and gentle teaching of my daughter, and talk with you more about condom use. I chose the last, for Pamela really enjoyed you and you seemed to be a really nice guy and a caring lover, and just as she had volunteered, she and I would have wanted no one else to have been her first.

I recalled my first and I thought I wished he had been you… and that was the thought that got me in trouble. I had stopped to drink some iced tea and as I set the glass down, you looked deeply into my eyes and said I was even more beautiful than my daughter. You continued to tell me everyone needed to have a very special mom like me. I could not stop looking at you as your locking eyes seemed to caress me in that special spot in my mind and then reached in and knew. Yes it would be illegal, and it might be morally wrong, but I wanted to know what you knew that would make me feel as good as you were making my recently virginal daughter feel!

You finally let my eyes go and then I realized you had boldly taken my hand in yours and was softly caressing my palm and fingers very sensuously. I was turned on more than I'd ever been in my life! Although I knew I had to get out of this,

I just didn't want to. I thought. Why
hasn't Pamela returned? Then, I
remembered she had gone with a girlfriend
to the next town to swim all day and
wouldn't be back till 6 when my husband
would pick them up and bring them home.

As you caressed my hand, it was 10 in
the morning--what could you do with me
until 4, I thought? I cleared my head of
that very dangerous but exciting thought.
I said nothing, but I gently moved my
hand away, as I got up to get more tea
for the two of us.

"I could throw you out," I thought,
"But I'd already made my decision to let
you be with my daughter."

I focused on that and returned to
protection. I covered the same ground
again and got the same answer that those
things were not the problem, but you
were. It was so hot that day that our
clothing was getting soaked with sweat. I
saw a perfect large banana lying on the
side counter. I got up to get it and said
that we should be sure. I started to sit
down and take some condoms out of my
purse which was on the table, but then I
remembered that we were in a sweat box. I
said it was so hot in here we should go
to my air conditioned bedroom and show
you how to use a condom. I about fainted
as I said it, and realized all the
meaning it could have. I remember
wondering what meaning it held for you.

I asked you to follow me, and we went
down the hall to my bedroom. I sat down
on the bed by my nightstand and asked you
to sit by me. I opened the drawer and
took out four condoms, and handed them to
you. I reached over you to lay the banana

on your other side because you were very
close to me. When I was doing it, I
glanced into your lap and you were hard,
thick and down your jeans leg and at the
end, your jeans were soaked. Must be
sweat, I thought, couldn't be anything
else. I returned to sanity, sort of. Then
I suddenly remembered I'd had only one
larger lover before, and although
interesting, in a curiosity way, once had
been more than enough, for he thought his
size was all I needed. I was never with
him again. Come to think of it, he
claimed he couldn't use condoms, and that
day I was about to start my period and
nothing happened even though I let him
finish in me. I think when I looked in on
you and Pamela, her first time, I didn't
really look at all of you, for I was
thinking of Pamela.

I got back to sanity again and I asked
you to tear off one of them, then open it
properly and then pretend the banana was
you and properly roll the sheath on while
pinching the top to maintain a small
space for the fluid. You did it
perfectly.

I said, "Do another one, and you did."

Then I did one to show you what a
woman might do wrong. Watch for her nails
on opening and rolling it on by hand or
mouth I said--do be particularly careful
of nails in maintaining the space at the
end with no damage. As I did it, I
thought how lazy my husband had become.
Although it was he who didn't want any
more 'kids,' he expected me to prepare
him either with hand or mouth. I guess
this was a refresher for tonight or would
it be next week as it had been for a

month. I felt dampness in my panties and I excused myself to go to the bathroom.

"My period is coming up and I might have been a day or two early," I thought.

When I looked, it wasn't that, although there was a tiny hint of pink. I was starting, but this wetness was the liquid of excitement. I had become so excited I had soaked my panties and my shorts were soaked all the way through, and showing all over the crotch and beginning down the legs. My forbidden thoughts had me so excited and ready, I had lost my logical mind!

My cute new silk dressing gown was hanging on the bathroom door. It was very thin and cool. I didn't do it with premeditation, but I took off all my clothes and put on the cute little, thigh-length buttoned gown. I walked out and there you stood with the bed turned down and facing me. I startled and froze.

You asked, "Did I misunderstand? Did you not accept my invitation?"

I didn't answer. You walked to me and stood looking longingly in my eyes, caressed my face with those wonderful fingers of yours and asked me if I was sure I wanted you.

I whispered, "Yes."

Eric you removed my dressing gown, kissed me and told me how beautiful I was and how kind it was I had decided to be your 200th. You laid me down and kissed me, caressed me, touched me and explored me and all the while told me all the reasons at age 31, I was more beautiful than my daughter. You were magnificent and you spent the next 5 hours showing me that you had learned a great many things in your encounters and practice. I'd had those condoms in my purse for a reason, and after your first time breaking the 30 barrier and my first time being with a young lover, I returned them to the drawer and was never with my other man again. You met every need. Over the summer you continued with Pamela and with me, and I don't believe there could have ever been a more satisfied mother and daughter. With first hand experience, I did learn why the problem was you. Apparently, through the years, all of your lovers have chosen their own way.'

"Eric, when we moved at the end of summer, you told Pamela and me, you would remember us always, and you were sure you would see us again. You never forgot us and we never forgot you. We moved away at the end of that summer, and the next year, both of us had your babies. Two boys! Now both are 43 and they have a lot of children. You head huge families with both girls and boys. They are, so beautiful! You make good descendants!

*Desire Davidson*

# Sex by the Lines

Fall came and I decided to approach an attractive older woman again. I knew Mrs. 'W' (Janet) from her participation in my school plays. She assisted our English teacher with the sets and technical set up. Janet had a daughter my age, but I really didn't know her very well.

Our English teacher was sick around the time we were supposed to be running lines for the upcoming play and my opposite actress was sick that week as well; so Janet ran lines with me. She was funny, personable, bright, and cute. She told me she was 35 years old and I was going to find some way to seduce her.

Janet had green eyes and long brown hair. She was cute; her personality just made me want her more. She had a perfect C-cup and great legs. She tended to wear short skirts, and when she was working on a ladder placing a set, I caught a quick glimpse of her long shapely legs.

I found my opening. I faked having trouble memorizing my lines and asked if she could help me after school. She agreed. It was the perfect day. School was out early for some maintenance work, her daughter Jean Ann was in the band and they had gone on an overnight band competition. Her husband was a salesman and he was on the road for the week. We couldn't run lines at school because of the electrical maintenance, so Janet took me home with her.

Circumstances could not have brought me a better opportunity if I had the power to control all these events.

We sat at her kitchen table for a while and had some hot tea to drink and then after about an hour of running lines at the table, we moved to the sofa in the family room. She sat down first and I sat down as close to her as possible without spooking her. I was very mature for my age, looked older and I was taller than Janet. I was determined to seduce this lovely woman.

Janet had on a tight v-neck sweater top and its turquoise color was a striking contrast to her cream colored linen skirt. She was wearing heels that matched her sweater and she was a living doll.

We were running lines for my part, and I noticed she put a pillow behind her back and grimaced.

I said, "Janet is your back hurting?"

She replied, "My back is killing me. I twisted it setting a piece of scenery yesterday and today my back is all knotted up."

"I'm sorry you're in pain--should I go?"

"No, don't go, we need to finish your lines." she said.

"Is there anything that eases you?" I asked.

Janet replied, "I only get relief when I'm lying on my back."

I suggested that we lie down and continue running lines. We went down the hall to her bedroom and lay down on her bed.

I said, "This room is beautiful."

She said, "I decorated it myself."

Even though Janet was lying down, she was still complaining of her back. I suggested I give her a massage and see if that would give her some relief.

"A massage might work," she said.

Janet went to her closet and got a thin short silky robe and went in the bathroom and changed out of her clothes. When she came back, I had removed all of my clothes except for my boxer shorts and I caught her looking at the very noticeable bulge down the right leg of my boxers before she lay face down.

She told me where her back hurt and I moved beside her and began to rub the affected area. After a while, I straddled her hips and provide a more efficient massage. It felt to me that she had neither a bra nor panties on under the robe. After I worked the knots out of her back, I lay down beside her and she moved onto her back. My cock was rock hard from the stimulation of seeing her and feeling her body through her silky robe.

Janet stretched out her arms in a long satisfying stretch and said the massage was wonderful. When she brought her arms down again to the bed, her right arm accidentally touched my hardness. She looked over and saw the outline of my hard cock. I was already much larger than most grown men and was still growing. Janet looked in fascination at my cock's outline in the boxers.

She said, "You scamp, are you about to get off on me?

I replied by taking her hand and placing it on my cock. Janet held it through the fabric and I reached for her firm breasts and big nipples through the open v-neck of the silky robe.

I said, "Janet I want to make love to you!"

There was a long awkward pause; then she stood up and took off the robe as I pulled off my boxers. We returned to the bed and I began kissing her and fondling her breasts as she stroked my cock and realized I was significantly bigger than her husband. She reached in the night stand and brought out a condom package and tore it open and tried to put it on my big cock. It was hopeless, the first broke as she attempted to roll it on and the second only covered about 6 inches of my thick cock before it broke too.

Janet said, "Forget the condoms; I really want you to cum in me anyhow."

I moved between her legs and found she was not ready for me, so I lay between her legs and gave her the best kiss of all as I tongued her clit until she came several times. The stimulation caused her to grow wet and relaxed and she took my cock and guided it into her.

"God! You're big," she said.

"You have just the perfect slit to handle it," I replied.

Her pussy felt great when I was fully in her. I allowed her to adjust to my thickness and length and then I began to fuck her. We fucked for more than ten minutes and at about the five minute mark Janet began to come on my cock and kept it up until I exploded and filled her pussy with my cum.

I moved out of her still hard and I fondled her breasts and kissed her in the afterglow of the moment.

"She said, "When you came in me you pulsed over an over again, I must be full of your come."

"I'll take care of that," I said

I doubled a pillow under my head and asked her to straddle my face so I could eat my warm cum out of her pussy and bring her to one marvelous orgasm after another. After awhile she moved down my body and impaled her firm body on my cock and took me in the woman astride position. She rode furiously and I felt her strong orgasms squeeze my cock over and over. She brought me to the brink of coming several times and then finally I shot streams of cum into her body again.

She said, "Eric that was wonderful, I've never come like that!"

She moved beside me and laid her head on my hairy chest. I traced her pretty full lips with my finger tip and told her how beautiful she was.

I asked' "How is your back now?"

She said, "With all those orgasms, I don't feel a thing. I'll take you as my pain reliever regularly."

Janet moved up and kissed me with long passionate kisses. I knew it was getting late and although she had a fully open schedule, I did not. I asked her what time it was and she looked at the clock radio and told me it was just after 5 pm. I had to go then. In the next few days, we found ways to be in each others arms three times.

Later in November, I was with her another seven times and every time was better than the last as we learned to better pleasure each other.

*Desire Davidson*

# Susan's Twister Party

It was time for one of Susan's sex parties. She said it would have a 'twist' when she called me. With Susan in charge that could mean anything. She told me not to bring a date because she would have a girl friend for me. I'd never been disappointed by Susan's selection and I was sure her choice would be perfect.

Susan's parties always had a sexual theme and always resulted in four men pairing off with four women and going to their separate bedrooms to spend two hours having sex. Occasionally there was an inter-bedroom swap after the first hour, but all sex was behind closed doors.

I arrived at the party and Susan introduced me to my date for the evening--Sandy Mc...

Sandy was a cute red head and well built. Sandy was a senior at the University of Oklahoma. I fixed some snacks for us and sat down on a couch in the game room with Sandy. After we finished our snacks I began to kiss Sandy gently and romantically but the cute little doll very quickly stepped up the pace to passionate kisses. Her full lips drew me to her. As we kissed I stroked her face and hair and gently explored her legs.

At 8:30 pm Susan left her date's embrace and went to each couple announcing that we were going to play 'Strip 21' for a party game. This was something new. We gathered around her table and she had four decks of cards.

Tim and Debbie took turns shuffling and
cutting the cards. The rules were simple:
the dealer (Susan) dealt two cards to the
guest and two to herself. The guest then
decided if they would stand pat or make
21 through a third requested card. Susan
made the same decision. If Susan won,
then the guest had to remove the number
of clothes equal to the difference of
their hand and 21. This very rapidly left
all eight people totally naked. Susan
then had each of the girls and guys draw
a number to pair us off at random. In our
case, Sandy and I ended up together. We
and the others proceeded to the couches
to continue making out until time was
called.

Sandi had large beautiful nipples
which got lots of attention from me. She
was a real redhead-a pretty matching trim
covered her swollen pussy lips. I moved
my hand from her soft legs and separated
her labia with my fingers and found she
was lubricated and totally relaxed. My
finger settled on her clit and as we made
out I proceeded to bring her to eight
orgasms in twenty minutes. As I played
with her, she gauged my cock's size and
length as she stroked it with her
talented hand. Susan called time at the
hour.

We gathered around again and she
announced that one couple was going to
play a game called 'Twister' before we
went to our bedrooms. To select the
couple to play, she had 12 cards and
dealt three to each couple. Whoever had
high cards would play the game. Sandy and
I had a winning hand and everyone else
had nothing--I'm sure Susan had stacked

the deck to insure Sandy and I were the couple to play the game.

Susan spun the dial around the positions on the game wheel and Sandy and I assumed them on the large colored dots on the plastic sheet on the floor. Our naked bodies made contact as we moved into positions and my cock was hard as rock and was seeping pre-cum. The last spin had Sandy down on her hands and knees and I on my knees immediately behind her. The head of my hard cock actually parted the swollen outer lips of her cunt in this position.

Susan asked, "Sandy do you want to do it?"

Sandy said "Yes!"

Susan asked, "Do you want a condom?"

Sandy said, "No, I want to feel his big cock shoot cum in me."

I immediately placed my hands on Sandy's hips and thrust my cock into her wetness. A roar of approval went up from the other six people and I increased my pace of fucking her. After about five minutes she started coming on me.

When she caught her breath she said, "I want to keep fucking but I want to be on my back." I pulled out of her and a long stream of clear excitement dripped from my unsatisfied cock.

Her pretty trimmed red bush glistened with our wetness.

Susan brought two quilted comforters and a pillow and Sandy lay down on them. Her beautiful red hair fanned out on the pillow. I leaned over her and kissed her full lips.

I said, "Sandy this is going to be special."

As I looked into her green eyes I positioned myself between her pretty legs and she took hold of my cock and placed the head in her swollen cunt lips. Sandy was really a 'fire cracker' for as I thrust into her she wrapped her legs around my back and came for the second time and kept coming. She was as big an exhibitionist as I.

We continue to fuck for about five minutes when the others began a chant for me to come in her. I did just that, shooting stream after stream of cum into her body. Again she came at the same time, crying out with me as we took each other.

I pulled out of her and was still hard and ready for another go. My white, creamy, cum oozed out of her cunt.

Sandy looked at me and said, "It appears that you are still ready; I am too. I want to ride you."

I lay down beside her on my back and Sandy straddled my body and guided my cock back into her wet cunt. In this 'woman astride position' she angled her torso toward my chest maximizing my cock's contact with her clit. The other couples cheered us on as Sandy flexed her legs to rise just so the head of my cock was in her and then thrust all the way down its shaft. She had only been riding me for about three minutes when she began to have chain orgasms, one orgasm after another. This girl was phenomenal.

Our watchers were ready to start their own sessions and they began to chant come, come, come, come …

As Sandy plunged down on my cock, she said "Now!" and both of us came together.

My cock again filled her pussy with cum. We lay joined for a time as she lay on my chest. Then she lay down beside me and I pulled her to me so I could kiss her and fondle her breasts. Shortly we realized the other six people had gone off to their bedrooms while we remained in each other's arms enjoying the afterglow of sex.

Sandy and I got up and went down the hall to the bedroom with an open door. I led her into the bedroom and we lay down on our sides facing each other. I asked her if I could clean her up and give her a few more orgasms. I lay down on my back with a doubled pillow under my head. Then I asked Sandy to straddle my head. That placed her cunt right over my mouth as she held on to the headboard. I thrust my tongue into her, licking my warm cum from her pussy; then when she was cleaned up, I began to tongue her clit. In just a few minutes she began to have chain orgasms again. After about twenty minutes, she moved off me and lay beside me, almost exhausted, but she began fondling my cock and balls as I kissed her and sucked her nipples.

We talked about other things we would like to do with each other. I told her I'd like to 69 with her if my large cock wasn't too uncomfortable for her mouth.

"I'd like to come in your mouth and then French kiss with you and take the cum into my mouth," I said

She had something else in mind for a grand finale, but first we moved into a 69 position and proceed to lick and fondle each other. Shortly, she placed her lips around the head of my cock and began to suck. With each suck, Sandy pulled more of my big cock into her mouth. As I flicked her clit with my tongue, she proceeded to move her hand up and down on the upper shaft while swirling her tongue over the sensitive parts of the head. She began to come and I began to come. When I finished, I pulled away and moved up to her mouth to receive my cum back in a French kiss. The excess cum dribbled down both our chins due to the copious amount her expert mouth had pulled from my balls. I asked what she wanted to do now; we had about forty-five minutes left of our private party.

Sandy said, "Susan told me you have a selective bisexual side."

"Indeed I do."

"What did you have in mind?"

She said, "The one thing I have never done is to have anal sex."

I said, "Anal sex is both bisexual and heterosexual and I had considerable experience both ways."

She said, "That's what I want, an experienced man who is patient and gentle to introduce her to the act.

I leaned over and kissed her as my hand roamed over her firm breasts and her large nipples.

I always brought a small zippered bag with me when I came to Susan's parties. Inside were large condoms in case a partner didn't want me to come in her, as well as finger condoms, latex gloves, Vaseline and KY Jelly, and hand lotion.

"Sandy do you want me to introduce you bare back or do you want a condom?" I asked.

She said, "You silly man, my cunt is drenched with your cum and I want my ass to be the same!"

I went on and said, "We can do it spooned, you on hands and knees, or us face to face with your legs over my shoulders."

"I suggest the latter," I said, "I want to look into your beautiful green eyes as I fuck you.

It was so easy to bring her to orgasm with vaginal entry; I wanted to see if Sandy would come from having her ass fucked.

I asked her to lie on her side while I gently lubricated her anus and opened her with one finger, two fingers and then three, to make sure she could accommodate me. Then she rolled over and sat up and lubricated the head and shaft of my cock. She then turned on her back. I positioned myself between her beautiful freckled legs and lifted them onto my shoulders. She took my cock and placed it against her little relaxed hole. I eased the head of my cock into her, slowly opening her again as I'd done with my fingers. I stayed there applying steady pressure. As she relaxed I pushed into her past her sphincter muscle.

I asked, "Are you comfortable with my size."

She said, "Yes. Please go slowly."

I asked if I should go on and she said yes and I gently eased my cock into her until I bottomed out and my big balls were against her ass.

I didn't have to ask.

She said, "Fuck me now, I feel like I'm ready to come."

I gave her about a dozen full length
strokes and she began to come in those
long chain orgasms of hers. Her pulsating
canal felt like it was squeezing cum out
of me, so I began to shoot streams of cum
into this delicious little girl's ass.
When I finished filling her with cum I
stepped into the bathroom and wet a wash
cloth and came out and cleaned Sandy up.
Then I went back and urinated and cleaned
my cock so it was as clean as at the
start of the evening. As I handled my
cock to clean it, the texture of the
washcloth and the slipperiness of the
soap and the use of a towel to rough dry
it stimulated me to have another raging
hard on. I walked back into the bedroom
and Sandy took a turn in the bathroom.

When Sandy came back she asked, "How
much do you come when you ejaculate?"

I said, "Find out."

I got some lotion from my bag and told
her to apply it to my cock and jack me
off. I lay flat on my back while she sat
beside me and stroked my cock with her
soft hand. A few minutes passed and I
told her I was about to come and she
picked up the pace. Suddenly she cried
out "Oh my God!"

The first stream of white, creamy, cum
shot out of my cock and hit directly in
her face; as did the successive shots.
Her pretty mouth and nose was covered in
cum. There was even a pearl strand in her
beautiful, dark red hair.

I sat up and took her into the
bathroom and showed her in the mirror the
pretty pearl necklace in her hair.

Sandy said, "I've never been with
anyone who came that much."

I said, "I've met a few others in my life, and I was sure she eventually would meet them too.

I took a fresh washcloth and cleaned her face and wiped the cum out of her hair and. We then returned to the bedroom and lay on the bed on our sides facing each other and talking about how good we were together. We fondled each other for a while, and then returned to long passionate kisses.

Hearing Susan's bell ringing, we got up and dressed and returned to the game room for refreshments before going our separate ways.

*Desire Davidson*

# Three Girls at the Lake

I never drink. I never have--it affects sexual performance. Maintaining high sexual performance has been central to my life as a sex addict. But I do associate with people who do drink.

One summer I had two friends Kent and Tim. They too were not shy in a group sex situation. They frequently went out with Vicki and Debbie. I had a frequent date in Cynthia who lived in Shawnee. I had yet to have sex with her, but tonight was to be the night.

I was setting up the party so I was bringing everything needed for a good time. Kent and Tim claimed to be great beer drinkers. When I cooked this party up, Kent and Tim gave me thirty dollars with the instruction to buy Colt 45 Malt Liquor, a high alcohol content beer.

The evening of the party, each us of brought our girl and met at a beautiful grassy spot by the lake. We had six quilts to make a big padded area. Cynthia and I arrived first and had the beer in a tub of ice cooling down for the rest of the party.

When the others arrived, a beautiful sunset stretched across the lake's horizon. I had built a fire to give light for our romantic doings. Tim and Kent immediately began to hit the cold beer. Cynthia and I were making out as were the others as the sun set and twilight set in.

Debbie was with Tim. She was a very small girl about 4'8' and was really cute and popular as head cheerleader.

Vicki was with Kent. Vicki was a fire twirler for the football half time band. She too was cute and popular and was about 5'6" and had beautiful legs.

I had not yet had sex with the three girls so it would be a first entry in my sexual encounter log.

The night was beginning to enfold us, so I lit a Coleman lantern which in addition to the fire provided enough light for everyone's taste for voyeur and exhibitionist. In the make out session shirts and blouses and bras had already been discarded. The girls had great breasts. Debbie's breasts were about the size of a champagne glass. Vicki's were a solid C-cup as were Cynthia's. Debbie had surprisingly large nipples-like an old fashioned first grade pencil eraser. The others' nipples were smaller even though they had larger breasts. Tim and Kent were on the verge of being drunk and were about to learn alcohol and sex don't always mix and always makes for poor performance.

Tim stood up and stripped off his jeans and shorts and was fully naked in the glow of the lantern and fire light. He had Debbie stand up and he took her shorts and panties off. Debbie was a natural blond. I had started the fire when we first arrived and the additional light of the fire made it possible to see Debbie's nipples were quite erect and Tim's cock was quite limp.

Kent took his shorts and Jockeys off and encouraged Vicki to do the same. She had long blond hair that partially covered her breasts when swept forward. Kent was in the same shape as Tim, with a limp cock and still he was drinking. The guys thought they needed more of a make out session and proceeded with that.

When I had finished adding wood to the fire, I returned to Cynthia and found her nude waiting and ready for me. I pulled down my pants and removed my underwear to liberate my cock which was long and . thick, hard as a rock and ready for action. I lay down beside Cynthia and turned my attention to her lovely breasts and she began to stroke my cock. She said, 'I want to try to suck it' Cynthia knelt and I stood. She pulled my cock down away from my belly and proceeded to lick the swollen purple head like a lolly pop. I was watching the others and Vicki and Debbie were doing the same to their respective guys but weren't having much luck in getting their guys hard-they had already drunk too much. Cynthia began to inch her lips over the head of my cock and was doing quite well sucking me off when I stopped her and had her lay down so I could eat her delicious pussy. I thrust my tongue into her labia and arrived at her clit. She had a surprisingly long clit and I was sure this little fire cracker was going to pop with a little tongue action. Indeed she did, coming hard, three times in succession, as I continued to lick her. I moved up to her face and she turned on her side to face me. Her lovely auburn hair framed her face as she again reached for my cock and proceeded to give long slow strokes with her pretty hand. In a few minutes Cynthia said she would like me to make love to her. I asked if she wanted a condom and she said no, that she was on birth control pills and wanted to feel me come in her. I glanced over at the others and I thought I heard either Tim or Kent snore. Debbie and Vicki were talking to each other and there was no action for them.

Cynthia moved onto her back with her pretty long legs bent at the knees. Her soft deep auburn hair flowed across the pillow. I had brought for her. She too matched--my baby was a natural. I moved between her legs and she took my cock and guided it into her as I moved forward to enter her. She was wet and ready from our making out and having come three times by oral sex. I gently eased into her allowing her vagina to accommodate my larger cock. She was very tight and felt great. She raised her legs over my back and locked them. In a minute or two she told me to fuck her because the suspense was killing her. I began to move back and forth in her and increased the pace of thrusting as she encouraged me. I fucked her for about ten minutes and she began to come on me. Cynthia's long clit was making contact with my shaft on every stroke.

At about the 15 minute mark, I caught her coming and began to shoot stream after stream of white creamy cum into her body. I finished coming and was still hard, so I continued rapid thrusting as she continued to come. Finally she said that was enough-she couldn't withstand another orgasm.

I lay down beside Cynthia and kissed deep kisses with her, as my fingers stroked her delicious nipples. I had my back turned to the others and did not know of their approach, but suddenly I felt four hands on my back and buttocks. They announced their arrival by saying they had been watching as we fucked and wanted to join the party. They said their dates were passed out drunk and useless. I looked at Cynthia and she didn't object.

I started to make out with Vicki and my cock became fully erect as I stroked her beautiful legs.

Vicki was an excellent kisser. After a long kissing and breast fondling session, I placed her on her back and thrust my tongue into her. Her clit was small and I didn't expect she would come through vaginal intercourse, so I was particularly attuned to giving her as many orgasms as possible with my tongue. After about 10, I told her that was my limit. My excited cock was seeping pre-come and was hard and ready. She kissed and licked the head of my cock as if mesmerized by my size. I asked if she wanted a condom. She said no, I want all of you just like Cynthia had.

Vicki wanted to be on her back so I could fondle her breasts and suck her nipples. I moved between her legs and she took my cock and positioned the head in her wet, ready cunt. I gently eased in, allowing her to adjust to my larger cock. When I was fully in, I began a gentle in and out motion. Suddenly I saw in her eyes a look that told me she wanted more. She cried out, "Fuck me cowboy, fuck me!"

She was loud enough to be heard at distant camp sites. I fucked her long and hard and she came long and hard. I now know that I was aggressively rubbing her 'G-spot.' and she was very orgasmic that way. I filled her up with cum. As I pulled out of her cunt, cum dripped out of her and puddled on the quilt. I moved down beside her and pulling her to me, I told her how good she was and had a long kissing session with her.

Debbie, the little blond firecracker, was rubbing my cock as Vicki and I were kissing. Soon she said, "I think it's my turn big boy; your cock is as hard as a rock." I left Vicki and turned to Debbie. I told her it would be best if she took a ride in the 'partner astride position' so she could control the penetration. I lay down on my back and as Debbie came down, Cynthia took my cock and positioned the head inside Debbie's pussy lips; then continued to hold it while she moved onto me. She was wet and ready from watching but still had a difficult time sliding down on to me fully. He little pussy was stretched to the limit. She just set on me for a minute or two fully adjusting to the girth and length. Then she began to rise and fall--impaling herself on me in ever quickening strokes. The little minx began to come after five minutes of the ride and she must have come a dozen times before I filled her little body with cum. She pulled off of me and I could see the white cream dripping from her pussy. I reached over and got the pillow and doubled it and put it under my head and asked Debbie to come straddle my face. I ate her delicious little blond cunt for about fifteen minutes. I lost count how many times the sexy little bitch-in-heat came.

I was still eating Debbie's cunt when I felt someone mount my fresh erection. She slid onto my cock and began to pleasure her self with it. I couldn't tell whether it was Cynthia or Vicki thrusting onto my cock. It was exciting not to know who was fucking me. Debbie dismounted my face after about 20 minutes of continuous coming. The girl riding me was also coming and I joined her by shooting my cum into her body. I had just filled Cynthia.

Cynthia, Vicki, Debbie, and I spent the night doing all kinds of girl on guy, girls on guy and some girl on girl and some girl on girl on guy while fully penetrated and laying back on my chest. Eventually my cock did soften but my tongue mouth and fingers continued to keep the girls happy throughout the night. What of Tim and Kent--they never woke up until the dawn. Don't drink and make love.